A
Prospect
of
Flowers

A BOOK ABOUT WILD FLOWERS

ANDREW YOUNG

VIKING

VIKING

Penguin Books Ltd, Harmondsworth, Middlesex, England
Viking Penguin Inc., 40 West 23rd Street, New York, New York 10010, U.S.A.
Penguin Books Australia Ltd, Ringwood, Victoria, Australia
Penguin Books Canada Ltd, 2801 John Street, Markham, Ontario, Canada L3R 1B4
Penguin Books (N.Z.) Ltd, 182–190 Wairau Road, Auckland 10, New Zealand

First published by Jonathan Cape 1945
Published by Viking 1985

Copyright 1945 by Andrew Young

Typeset in VIP Bembo

Typeset, printed and bound in Great Britain by
Hazell Watson & Viney Limited,
Member of the BPCC Group,
Aylesbury, Bucks

BRITISH LIBRARY CATALOGUING IN PUBLICATION DATA

Young, Andrew, *1895–1971*
 A prospect of flowers.
 1. Wild flowers—Great Britain
 I. Title
 582.13'0941   QK306

ISBN 0–670–80345–6

Contents

	Acknowledgements	7
1	How It Began	9
2	The Year's First Flower	12
3	Trees and Shrubs in March	20
4	Buttercups and Lilies	28
5	Names of Spring Flowers	38
6	A Simple Method	46
7	Spring Herbs	52
8	Trees and Shrubs in May	63
9	The Fear of Flowers	75
10	Botanists and Botanophils	83
11	June Orchids	90
12	A Good Guide	97
13	Flowers	105
14	A Confession	112
15	The Morals of Plants	118
16	Poets' Botany	136
17	Some Difficulties	145
18	Plants and People	152
19	Eve and Linnaeus	162
20	Types of Botanist	171
21	Sketches	177
22	A Scottish Rhapsody	186
23	The Fall	197
24	The Year's Last Flower	204
	Apologia	211

Illustrations are from John Gerard:
Herball or Generall Historie of Plantes (1597).

Acknowledgements

Friends I have to thank for helping me with this book are Viola Meynell, Sir Edward Marsh, F. A. Voigt, John Arlott and John Allan of the British Museum. F. A. Voigt I have also to thank for publishing several chapters in *The Nineteenth Century*, and Sir Edward Marsh for correcting the proofs.

1   How It Began

One morning my mother came into my room and asked how it was that I had sand in my boots. How indeed, if I had been to school the day before?

To play truant, to spend a long day with nothing to do, was no easy task; I should have been happier at school; but it was a matter of principle. Few boys nowadays, I suppose, sit late at night reading *Amadis of Gaul* or *Palmerin of England* by the light of a candle stuck in an empty wine-bottle. (What books those were – and still are!

Tenebror had his armour green, whereon was figured many golden poppies, and in his shield he bare Troy Town.)

But the Romantic was a potent idea in the later years of Queen Victoria, and to play truant seemed romantic. Of course there was a grave risk; when the Rector at School-Prayers next morning read that passage from Scripture full of Woes – 'Ye serpents, ye generation of vipers' – his favourite passage when he was bad-tempered about something – I gave myself up for lost. But it was the risk that was romantic. The shade of Sir Walter Scott drove me to play truant from his own school.

But how was I to fill in the day? Clearly I could not be seen walking up and down Princes Street. If boys still play truant, they must regard picture-houses as a kind of divine blessing, for there, shaded from inquisitive eyes, they can pass many pleasant hours. But there were no picture-houses in those days when boys wore boots. We learn from *Marmion* that when young Walter Scott played truant he went bird-nesting on Blackford Hill; and as he had an uncle, Dr John Rutherford, who was Professor of Botany in Edinburgh, he may also have looked for wild flowers; but I had little interest in birds and none at all in wild flowers. I visited the National Art Gallery and the Museum of Scottish Antiquities, but soon exhausted their possibilities. My chief resort became what were called Italian ice-cream shops. Some years later, when I was a student, I was pitted against the champion cake-eater of Aberdeen University, the loser to pay the bill, a large one, as it included tea and cakes for all the spectators; I was not the loser, though returning that evening to Edinburgh I had to stand in the corridor of the train. But if I was gifted with a good digestion, Heaven knows that to spend a whole day passing from one Italian ice-cream shop to another was beyond my power. So hard necessity drove me at last to try the country.

I had grown up to hate the country. As a child I had been taken for long country walks, which coincided for the most part with high stone walls. The gentry about Edinburgh had a peculiar

Veronica vera & maior.
Fluellen or Speedwell.

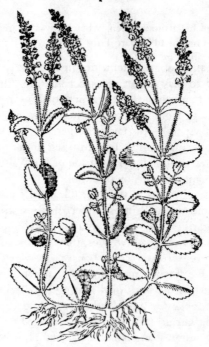

idea of property, enclosing it with these high walls, as though they were lunatics or a menagerie. I might have said with Mrs Millamant,

> I nauseate walking; 'tis a country diversion; I loathe the country and everything that relates to it;

but I could not have added with her,

> I hate the town too.[1]

But now, driven to seek refuge in the country, I began to have a sneaking regard for it, even a liking, as though I too, like little Matthew Arnold in his cradle,

> Was breathed on by the rural Pan.[2]

In fact by the time I had reached the top form of the Royal High School, I had become

> Dame Nature's pupil of the lowest form.[3]

As for the sand in my boots, it came from Cramond, a hamlet on the Firth of Forth. But I brought home more than sand, a wild flower. Seeing a pretty blue flower I stopped a countryman and asked its name; he told me it was Forget-me-not. If he had said anything else I should have believed him, but Forget-me-not was the one flower with which I was familiar. As a child I had seen it woven round Scripture-texts hung on walls, and it was the favourite decoration of such books as *Sandford and Merton* and *When Greek Meets Greek*. Not believing him I picked a flower and pressed it in a lesson-book. I showed it to several people, but there appeared to be no one in Edinburgh who had seen such a flower. At last a friend of my sister told me it was a Speedwell.

Speedwell, name of happy omen! It sped me on a long journey, from the sand-dunes of Norfolk to the cliffs of Cornwall, from the bogs of the New Forest to the mountains of Angus.

---

1. Congreve: *The Way of the World*.
2. 'Lines Written in Kensington Gardens'.
3. Wordsworth: 'The Excursion'.

2   The Year's First Flower

One wet January night, walking down to Swanage, I was aware of a flowery smell, and though like Keats I could not see what flowers were at my feet, I knew it came from Winter Heliotrope. This alien plant forms many colonies in the South, maintaining or even extending them by a thick mat of leaves. It is called Heliotrope because its flowers, purple-grey and scented, resemble the true Heliotrope's, and Winter from its strange habit of blooming in December or January. Is this the last flower of the old year or the first of the new?

Perhaps it is foolish to speak of a last and first flower, when some small plants, such as Chickweed, Groundsel and Shepherd's-purse, are always in bloom. Like sparrows they are with us through the year, and like sparrows they keep mostly to the haunts of men. They can pick up an easy living where the ground has been manured and turned over. As they are quick growers and freely pollinate themselves, generation follows generation so fast that they defy the gardener's hoe. Poorly protected in themselves, they manage by this kind of birth-rate to survive in the war on weeds. We call them weeds, not because they are wild, but rather because they are not; they are plants of cultivation, that followed man and his plough from the East. Such plants – there are many of them – may be unknown in a wild state, their original ancestors having died out. We call them weeds also because they are unattractive. Chickweed, as a relation of the beautiful Stitchwort, may at one time have had a larger flower, but seeking little or no help from insects, ceased to take a pride in its appearance; now it is Chickweed or Hen's Inheritance, mainly of interest to small birds and poultry. Groundsel interests only those who keep canaries. Yet Culpeper, who claims in his *Herbal* to have consulted *Dr Reason* and *Dr Experience* and also *Mr Honesty*,

a stranger in our daies,

greatly admires it.

Lay aside our learned Receipts,

he says;

this Herb alone shall do the deed for you in all hot diseases, and it shall do it, 1 Safely 2 Speedily.

Probably it is of ancient repute, for its name, which is Saxon, means a poultice. If Shepherd's-purse is named from its seed-pods, it follows Iago's advice and puts money in its purse. Like a shepherd it is hardworking and thrifty, boring deep with its thirsty tap-root and pressing its leaf-rosette against the ground to preserve the underlying moisture; unlike a shepherd it makes its fortune, storing its purses with many seeds, and leaving a rich legacy in the soil to the ungrateful gardener. But perhaps the name has nothing to do with money, for Coles (who in his *Art of Simpling* says of Culpeper,

he understood not those Plants he trod upon)

explains that the name was given

because the Seeds of it resemble the letherne bagge, wherein Shepherds put their Victuals.

These small plants are as clever as sparrows, or at least as efficient. 'See how we multiply and replenish the earth,' they say. Each might claim to be the year's first flower, or its last; but

Crowds see no magic in the trifling thing;
Pshaw! 'tis a weed![1]

As for Winter Heliotrope, perhaps we should think it belongs to the new year, for its relations, Butterbur and Coltsfoot, bloom in spring. Butterbur, growing by tree-shaded streams, is remarkable for its Rhubarb-like leaves. Botanists call it Petasites, the Hat-wearer, comparing them with the broad-brimmed hats worn by Greek peasants. They wore their hats to keep off the sun, this Petasites seeks to catch it. Most plants that grow in shady places have large leaves, such as Ferns, Wild Garlic and Lily of the

1. Clare: 'The Voice of Nature'.

Valley; they serve not only to absorb the sunlight, but also to evaporate the abundant water drawn through the roots. What a butterfly has to do with butter is unknown even to the *Oxford Dictionary*, but probably Coles is right when he explains,

> Butterburre was so called because the countrey Housewives were wont to wrap their Butter in the large leaves thereof.

Coltsfoot – Winter Heliotrope is sometimes called Scented Coltsfoot – is also named from its leaves, shaped like a young horse's hoof. Yet people, seeing the flower, might wonder at the name, for the flower is so precocious that it appears long before the leaves, though not so soon as that genius of the family, Winter Heliotrope. It looks naked without its leaves, especially when it grows in a stiff clay soil, often naked itself, because hated and shunned by most other plants. Lifted on a brown scaly stalk, it is closed and drooping at first, as though unwilling to awake; but a warm hour opens it to look up at the February sun. Its golden locks so quickly give place to grey hairs, disrespectfully scattered by the wind, that even in March we may think of autumn, though with an easy mind, as youth thinks of old age.

If Winter Heliotrope is too much an alien to be considered the year's first flower, what may we think of Snowdrop? Certainly its name has a wintry sound and it is a cold-looking flower. It hangs its head to protect the pollen from rain and sleet, and preserve its vital warmth. What makes it look like a drop of snow is the absence of a green calyx; most Lily-like flowers are without it, and in this case the absence may be useful, rendering the flower more conspicuous in a dim wood, especially to insects flying overhead. Bees visit the Snowdrop, eating honey in its white parlour; but like most spring flowers it cannot depend on being pollinated by insects. Usually it propagates itself by bulbs, a reason why it grows in clumps. It can therefore defy the storms that drive away its insect allies.

> Observe the faithful flowers! if small to great
> May lead the thoughts, thus struggling used to stand
> The Emathian phalanx, nobly obstinate;
> And so the bright immortal Theban band.[2]

2. Wordsworth: *Miscellaneous Sonnets*.

But as for its being truly wild anywhere – some botanists would shake their heads. Yet I have a good reason for maintaining it is wild in Arniston Woods. When Lady Dundas of Arniston was walking along Princes Street one February day, she was greeted by a hawker with 'Snowdrops fresh from Arniston Woods'. To be asked to buy her own Snowdrops was too much, and she closed her grounds. She believed they were wild, and perhaps they are; in any case, as she was kind enough to lend me a key, what can I do but uphold her belief?

As some doubt attaches to Snowdrop's nationality, we must consider the claim of other flowers, especially

> the rathe primrose that forsaken dies.[3]

(I imagined rathe meant late, till I learnt it had for its comparative the adverb rather.) But surely the rathe Primrose – we may see it before Christmas – is a regrettable sight. Coltsfoot closes and hangs its head in a storm, but how is a Primrose's flower protected? The leaves at least refuse to let water clog them and hinder their breathing; they carry it away in their wrinkles, and, sloping inwards, bear it in the right direction, towards the grateful roots. March is early enough for Primroses; when we imagine them,

> they come not single spies,
> But in battalions.[4]

I would sooner consider the claim of some poorer flower. There is Hairy Bitter-cress, attracting our attention by its habit of growing on mossy walls. It seems, however, to have an unfair advantage, for its leaves have been waiting all winter to give it a flying start in spring. Or there is Dog's Mercury. A well-stored rootstock gives it also a good start; but without some such start, in rootstock or bulb, few flowers could appear in spring. Annual Mercury, growing from a seed, will not appear till summer. But as Dog's Mercury is without petals, some people would hardly regard it as a flower. Or there is Moschatel, whose name, meaning musky, suggests that it hopes to attract a few flies. It reminds us that the race for the still empty earth is real, for so

3. Milton: 'Lycidas'.
4. *Hamlet.*

Cynocrambe.
Dogs Mercurie.

frail a plant could scarcely hope to survive in the crowded season. The Ivy-bloom, as the year's last flower, would stare in astonishment on its small relation, were its eyes not blind, or perhaps picked out by birds. Looking like a tiny clock-tower, Moschatel seems to enter the race as its own time-keeper. But we can hardly award so insignificant a flower the prize; we should be contradicting the botanists, who call it Adoxa, Without Glory.

If the competition were among leaves, not flowers, we might favour Cuckoo-pint. Or might we say its fresh leaves, forcing their way through the earth and shining in the February sun, are as good as flowers? It prepared for spring by storing its rootstock with so much food, that people used it to starch their ruffs and make a pudding called Portland Sago. But it will be a month or more before we see this Arum's flower, in shape at least like an

Arum Lily. Its purple spike, standing in a light green spathe, has gained it the name, Parson-in-the-Pulpit. The Parson's text will be from the *Song of Songs*: 'The flowers appear on the earth; the time of the singing of birds is come, and the voice of the turtle is heard in our land.' He will attract a congregation of small flies, but these, like the Children of Israel who hearkened not to the voice of Moses but lusted after the flesh-pots of Egypt, will be attracted more by a meaty savour. In fact they will be so inattentive to the sermon that, allured next by a scent of honey, they will wander down into the crypt-like part of the plant. But slanting hairs that allowed an easy descent to this Avernus forbid their return to the upper air. This is not meant to punish them for their inattention, but merely to make sure they are smeared with pollen. After a day or so the hairs are relaxed, and they fly away joyfully to seek another parson with as good a cellar. But, as the Parson's text says, 'the flowers appear on the earth'; Cuckoo-pint could not be the year's first flower.

Why should we not decide on Common Daisy, the first flower we are likely to see? Chaucer would approve, for to him it was

The emperice, and floure of flourès alle.[5]

We need not fear it will refuse the honour. Though Burns calls it

Wee, modest, crimson-tipped flow'r,[6]

the Daisy is not modest. Like an impudent juggler who spreads his mat in a crowded street, it spreads its leaf-rosette on the ground and, standing on it, defies interference from other plants. How could it be modest when we have named it Daisy, the Eye of Day? But perhaps we were thinking, not of an eye that opens, but of an eye that shuts. In the evening

Daisies button into buds,[7]

looking like white pitched tents; in fact, if the crimson tips are

---

5. *Legende of Good Women*.
6. 'To a Mountain Daisy'.
7. Clare: 'Summer Evening'.

for warmth, they are, so to speak, their own tent and fire. And, strangely enough, no flower has reminded poets more of death.

> I saw it – pink and white – revealed
>   Upon the white and green;
> The white and green was a daisied field,
>   The pink and white Ethleen.
>
> A sense that, in some mouldering year,
>   As one they both would lie,
> Made me move quickly on to her
>   To pass the pale thought by.[8]

Yet we might well say,

> I know not why thy beauty should
>   Remind me of the cold, dark grave.[9]

It ought to be a cheerful flower, this Bellis perennis, the Perennially Pretty,

> The constellated flower that never sets.[10]

And who ever saw a withered Daisy? One evening I sat at table in a company of botanists. They had been out all day after Brambles, not, as one might suppose, after Brambles to eat – I doubt if any of them had ever eaten a Bramble – but after what they called the Rubi, the Brambles of which there are more than a hundred species in this country. The talk at table was all about those Rubi, and I sat silent till it occurred to me that I too had a contribution to make to the subject. Turning to my neighbour I said, 'Do you know why Brambles are called Brumliekites in Cumberland?' 'No: why?' he asked. 'Because children eat so many that their kites or bellies rumble,' I replied. He looked at me with surprise, not so much, I imagined, at the information, as at myself. Somewhat piqued, I felt I had to assert myself, and turning to the company, I asked, 'Has anyone ever seen a withered Daisy?' The botanists seemed startled by the question; then, knowing I was not one of themselves, they smiled

8. Thomas Hardy: 'A Thought in Two Moods'.
9. W. H. Davies: 'The Daisy'.
10. Shelley: 'The Question'.

indulgently. As at that moment our host and hostess rose from the table, I never knew why they smiled, or why no one has ever seen a withered Daisy.

3 Trees and Shrubs in March

As the ancient Hebrews, like the modern Arabs, thought of a new day as beginning in the evening – 'the evening and the morning were the first day' – so they thought of a new year as beginning in autumn. Much can be said for this hopeful view, for no sooner are the trees rid of their leaves than catkins and buds are seen. As these are formed before the leaves fall, the new year might even be said to begin in summer. On the Alder, that clings to a riverbank – it leaves it only to clatter about a northern town as clogs – we notice the tight catkins and plum-coloured buds, the old female flowers, now like small hard cones, gaping at them in astonishment. All through winter the long tapering buds of the Beech have pointed to spring, but more noticeable are the pyramid-shaped buds on the thick Ash-twigs, for they are black, an unusual colour, perhaps warm for winter. But these last are the least reliable sign of spring, for more than any other tree

> the tender ash delays
> To clothe herself, when all the woods are green.[1]

They will still be closed when the children in my village wear them on Ash Wednesday, a practice they prefer to strewing ashes on their heads; a not inappropriate practice, for these mournful buds suit the Lenten season, the more so as they will burst into life at Easter.

A more trustworthy sign of spring is seen in the Common Elm. Elms are not social, at least not to the extent of forming woods like Oaks and Beeches. They may grow in clumps about a southern farm, 'huge homestead elms', a contrast to the northern farm's clump of Ashes, that provided spear-shafts in the

1. Tennyson: 'The Princess'.

gude days on the Border when there was neither peace nor justice heard of;[2]

but as often as not they stand alone. Such a lonely Elm on a ridge Matthew Arnold speaks of in 'The Scholar Gipsy', to Thyrsis and himself a 'signal tree'. Unfortunately this particular tree was not an Elm but an Oak.[3] But to anyone looking for spring every Elm is a signal tree; for

> Now ruddy are the elm-tops against the blue sky.[4]

Several trees and shrubs take on a reddish tinge in spring; the sharp-clawed shoots of the Briar have an angry hue, and the Silver Birch's claret-coloured twigs look strangely vinous against the snow-whitened hills. But the Elm's redness comes from its flowers. These appear so soon that even in March they may be replaced by their round-winged fruits, giving the tree a thickness that one might suppose was due to its bursting buds. Yet the fruits are so much barren waste. That its seeds are not good may mean merely that the tree has taken to using suckers instead, or it may be a reason for supposing it is not a native, another reason being its Latin name (Elm is from Ulmus). Not the same doubt attaches to the Wych Elm of the North, which produces good seeds, and has given its Celtic name to Loch Leven. The two trees are not always distinguished, but the Wych Elm has slightly larger leaves, which are also hairier, perhaps reminding us that an Elm is a near relation of the Stinging Nettle. And its leaves are more lop-sided, like a twisted heart; they might make us wonder, 'What! did the hand of Nature shake?' But their lopsidedness helps them to fall into a mosaic designed to catch the maximum amount of sunlight. Leonardo da Vinci noticed this arrangement:

> The leaves are arranged on plants in such a way that one covers another as little as possible, but they lie alternately one above the other as is seen with the ivy which covers the walls.[5]

Robert Bridges, who sees one sign of spring in the ruddy Elm-tops, sees another in the Larch

---

2. Westburnflat in *The Black Dwarf*.
3. *The Natural History of the Oxford District*.
4. Bridges: 'A Robin'.
5. *Note-books*.

The pale larch donneth her jewelry.[6]

Certainly the Larch has need to don something, if only the emeralds of its greening leaf-buds and rubies of its crimson flower-cones. Almost all conifers are evergreen; perhaps the Larch was evergreen once, for its seedlings are more or less so now; but in autumn it sheds its leaves and through winter presents a somewhat naked appearance. A plantation of Larches in winter might be mistaken for a wood of dead trees; in fact, when they are covered with grey lichen, as they commonly are, they look the ghosts of trees. But the pale Larch is quick to don its jewelry, even when the earth is still asleep, naked too, or with only a sheet of snow. The Larch is almost too active a tree; growing faster than most trees and shooting up straight and tall, it is apt to fall into the builder's hands and become, as it were, its own scaffold.

Anyone who sees the Larches that grow about Dunkeld, perched on inaccessible places, might suppose they were native trees; but the Birnam wood that came to Dunsinane was not of Larches. The Larch is no more a native than the Spruce Fir, which gives us our Christmas trees and, nowadays, frankincense as well. Apart from Yew and Juniper, our only native conifer is Scots Pine, often wrongly called Fir. (Pines are distinguished from Firs by their leaves growing, not singly, but in small bundles.) Scots Pines spread freely in some parts of the South, as on Bagshot Heath and about Bournemouth, but it is doubtful if they are indigenous; they are known to be native to only a few places in the North. Once abundant throughout Britain, as we see them now in Rothiemurchus Forest or by Loch Rannoch, they look like the thin straggling remnants of an army in far retreat. Yet no tree is more prodigal of its pollen; it turns yellow the calm creeks of a Highland loch. People have imagined it was fire and brimstone falling as on Sodom and Gomorrah, but to some small creatures it may seem manna from heaven. As for the Dunkeld Larches, they were introduced in the Eighteenth Century by the Duke of Atholl. One story says that, on receiving them as seedlings, he had them planted in a hothouse, where they quickly withered; flung out as dead on a rubbish-heap they

6. 'A Robin'.

revived in the colder air and flourished. The Larch is not a hothouse plant, but the best climber of northern mountains. Another story, to explain the inaccessible places where they grow, tells how the Duke, filling tin canisters with seeds, fired them from a cannon, and on the canisters bursting on the hillside the seeds were scattered. There is nothing original, of course, in the idea; a Gorse bush on a hot summer day can be heard firing its seeds like a minute machine gun. Lord Avebury tells how he put Herb Robert on the end of a billiard table, and that small red-coated infantryman shot seeds beyond the other end:

They were thrown from one end completely beyond the other, in some cases more than twenty feet.[7]

Certainly the Duke would be in a position to carry out the experiment, for alone among the King's subjects His Grace is allowed to keep a standing army.

The large trees of northern latitudes, with the splendid exception of Horse Chestnut, have small flowers, most of them being pollinated by the wind. Showy flowers, that attract insects, would be wasted on the wind,

> A rapid footless ghost,
> To offer whom a chair
> Were as impossible as hand
> A sofa to the air.[8]

Bacon in his *Sylva Sylvarum* even states that the Elm has neither flower nor fruit. The bigger the tree, the smaller the flower, might almost be said; so perhaps we see more evident signs of spring among the lesser trees and shrubs.

Richard Jefferies compared Blackthorn blossom to a white handkerchief beckoning to the sun. But before the blossom opens, we notice the keen colour of its buds, almost bursting with news of spring. At first they look like the brown seed-pearls that as a boy I shell-fished from the Tay; but while mine remained as they were, these pearls swell into large white gems, and soon, not content with being pearls, they break out into stars that powder the blackness of the hedge with a Milky Way. Poets

7. *Flowers, Fruits, and Leaves.*
8. Emily Dickinson (poems unnamed).

compare Blackthorn blossom to snow, and, sure enough, it melts
quickly in the sun; for in warm weather with plenty of insects
about, the flowers are soon fertilized and wither to a pinch of
untidy dust. We should pray for a cold spring if we want flowers
to last; yet not too cold, for if Blackthorn blossom leaves behind
the living seed, the frost, as though jealous for the melted snow,
may slay these innocents by their thousands. So where we saw in
spring the Blackthorn blossom put forth its leaf,

> Not with the golden fawnings of the sun,
> But sharpest showers of hail, and blackest frosts,[9]

we may find few Sloes in autumn. Some years Sloes are plentiful,
for, as the Greeks said, 'It is the year which bears and not the
field'; but as a rule they seem few compared with the abundance
of blossom, the penalty this shrub pays for awaking so early in
the year.

But the sun scarcely needs encouragement from the Blackthorn;
it was in January that the fisher-folk of Burghead burned the
clavie to encourage it to shine, and the sun in its turn has been
encouraging the trees. Perhaps it was in February that John
Freeman saw how the children

> broke the hazel boughs and wore the tassels
> Above their eyes – a pale and shaking crown.[10]

Hazel-catkins, clusters of male flowers, that hung on the twigs
all winter like small frozen worms, by March at latest lengthen
out and change to thin yellow caterpillars, suspended in such a
way as to be easily wagged by the wind. The tree is still bare of
leaves, otherwise the shaken-out pollen, caught on them, would
be unlikely to fall on the female flowers. These are minute and
partly hidden; few people notice their crimson stigmas waving
like a small sea-anemone from a fat bud. While the pollen of
insect-visited flowers is thick and sticky, making a lump of gold
on a bee's leg, the pollen that is carried by the wind is fine and
dry, buoyant on the air, and very abundant; even people in cities,
breathing the grass-pollen of distant meadows, are afflicted with
hay-fever. It is a 'fruitful cloud and living smoke'. I have seen a

9. Chapman: 'Charles, Duke of Byron'.
10. 'The Unloosening'.

girl, breaking off a Hazel-branch, almost disappear from sight, like Aphrodite in a golden cloud.

The Sallow's catkins come a little later, for observant of the Church's ritual, it waits to provide Palm for Palm Sunday. Willows often grow on a river-bank. It was by the rivers of Babylon the captive Jews hanged their harps upon the Willows; indeed, according to the legend, the boughs were so bent with the weight that now

> The willow weeps as in despair
> Amid her green dishevelled hair. [11]

Osiers grow in rushy beds, their shoots waiting to be woven into baskets, and larger pollards with knobbly heads, the stiff hair standing on end, serve to bind a river-bank with their roots. But Willows, Creeping and Alpine, grow on heaths and mountain-tops, trees about an inch high, as though they thought that, growing where they do, they were high enough already. The Sallow or Palm Willow grows anywhere, and early in March we may see in some sheltered spot, perhaps a hollow wood, as the first sign of spring, among Willows at least, 'the satin-shining palm'. By the end of March these buds have opened, the catkins on the male trees yellow with pollen,

> And through the leafless underwood rich stains
> Of sunny gold show where the sallows bloom. [12]

Most trees, being large plants with great reserves, can afford to be extravagant with their pollen and scatter it to the winds, but the Sallow, more careful of its gold, spends it on the entertainment of insects. Those who associate bees and moths with summer must be surprised to see them so busy. We could have no more convincing sign of spring:

> There the spring-goddess cowers in faint attire
> Of frightened fire. [13]

Even when Christmas snow lies softly on its spines, Gorse may be in flower and, with no bees about, deserve Goldsmith's description, 'unprofitably gay'. But this is an unreliable sign, for

11. George Darley: 'Sylvia'.
12. Clare: 'The Sallow'.
13. Bridges: 'The Palm Willow'.

is there not a proverb about the Gorse-flower and kissing being never out of season? Perhaps the proverb takes into account the two Autumnal Gorses, small shrubs that bloom late in the year. But the common Gorse's fire, though almost put out by the summer sun, never seems to die down completely; with a yellow spark left here and there, fresh flames are kindled and quickly spread, until by April the fire has covered a hill and there is no need to turn aside to see the great sight, a bush that burns and is not consumed. We need not take off our shoes like Moses; rather we are told, when we come to Whinny-muir,

> If ever thou gavest hosen and shoon,
> Sit thee down and put them on;[14]

or go on our knees like Linnaeus; yet we might do worse, for we shall see few greater sights.

In all these trees and shrubs the blossom comes before the leaves, in all but Gorse, whose leaves are only spines. But earlier still are the purple-grey leaves of Honeysuckle; we catch sight of them in a January wood, fluttering like strange butterflies in the cold wind. Matthew Green, a poet speaking of poets, says that in default of observation they indulge in fantasies; they

> Err with their wings for want of eyes.[15]

Honeysuckle or Woodbine has excited poets' wings as it excites the wings of Hawkmoths, hovering over it to lick the honey with their long tongues. So Herrick, in an invitation to Phillis, assures her

> The soft sweete Moss shall be thy bed,
> With crawling woodbine over-spread;[16]

while Shenstone tries to allure another Phillis by telling her

> Not a pine in the grove is there seen
> But with tendrils of woodbine is bound.[17]

But Honeysuckle does not crawl over moss, nor, even if it had tendrils, could it wind round a Pine.

14. 'Ballad'.
15. 'The Spleen'.
16. 'To Phillis'.
17. 'A Pastoral Ballad'.

> The woodbine, who her elm in marriage meets,
> And brings her dowry of surrounding sweets,[18]

must have contrived to entangle a stripling tree. Sir John Davies speaks more like a botanist (but not quite), when he compares Honeysuckle with a Paire of Garters, though the comparison comes oddly from the writer of that grave theological poem 'Nosce Teipsum':

> Go lovinge woode-bynde, clip with lovely grace,
> Those two sweet plants which beare ye flowers of love.

He knew at least that Honeysuckle can twine round a plant with a hurtful tightness, for he goes on with a lover's solicitude,

> Sweete bands, take heed lest you ungently bynd,
> Or with your strictnes make too deepe a print:
> Was never tree had such a tender rynd,
> Although her inward hart be hard as flynt.[19]

18. Churchill: 'Gotham'.
19. 'Upon a Paire of Garters'.

4   Buttercups and Lilies

A flora usually begins with the Buttercup family, and for that there appears to be a reason. 'Consider the Buttercup', says the botanist in effect; 'a simple plant, complete and distinct in all its parts, easy to examine'. But the beginner may feel that in his study of wild flowers he is being led up the garden path, for he finds that strangely different plants belong to this family, such as Columbine, Larkspur and Traveller's-joy. The explanation is that the botanist, a kind of Peeping Tom, regards the sex organs of plants rather than their general appearance, which is largely due to outward adaptations. But the beginner may find himself confused in another way; most of these plants are not complete and distinct in all their parts. Wood Anemone, with many others, has no petals, but has painted its sepals to take their place; Meadowrue, the Thalictrum of gardens, goes farther and gets rid of its sepals as well, giving its flowers an odd look, as though they were hardly flowers. In fact the family as a whole seems to have little idea what the various parts of a flower are for. The beginner might complain, How can I learn botany from plants that show so poor a knowledge of botany themselves? But what the botanist has in mind in recommending this family to the beginner is a common Buttercup.

Yet it is a knowledge of zoology rather than botany we might expect from plants called the Ranunculaceae or Family of Little Frogs. The name seems strange, when we think of Buttercups in dry meadows, or look at Traveller's-joy hanging on a tree, more like a serpent that might swallow a frog; but as often as not the members of the family live in damp places. Early in spring

> Horse-blobs stain with gold the meadow-drain,[1]

1. Clare: Sonnet.

or, as most poets call them, Kingcups or Marsh Marigolds. We are surprised to see them so soon, for damp places long continue chill, but we might be more surprised that they can grow in such places at all. Plants breathe in all their parts, even their roots, so that Corn will drown in half an inch of standing water. The farmer is careful to drain his fields, and usually we grow our indoor plants in porous pots with a hole at the foot. Marsh Marigold, however, like other stream-loving plants, is ventilated by air-channels that adapt it to a water-soaked soil. These make it soft and flabby to the hand, and the plant droops sadly if it has the misfortune to be picked. Soon too we shall see the pools covered with Water Crowfoot, a sheet of silver shaking in the wind. This Buttercup has completely taken to water, losing its hairs and bitter juice, no longer needed to protect it from land animals, and also its yellow colour, though it still keeps at its heart a speck of the ancestral gold.

Most early flowering plants prefer a wood; there, in a soil rich with decayed leaves, they find not only food but shelter,

> And in its green light smile their lives away.[2]

Or a hedge will serve; it is on the sunny side of a lane we get our first glimpse of Buttercup gold. In the South it may be Goldilocks, but everywhere it is more likely to be Lesser Celandine. If the petals are not fully unfolded, we notice that the undersides are a greenish brown, a colour that may protect the closed flower from night cold. Brown is a common colour in spring; an Oak with young leaves looks autumnal. Later, the open petals may have a bleached appearance, their gold changed to silver. Though so abundant and at one time much used as a medicine, this is the plant that Wordsworth strangely failed to recognize for 'thirty years or more', but about which he came to write three poems. It is not the plant carved on his monument at Grasmere; that is Greater Celandine, a kind of Poppy. Perhaps the sculptor thought its leaves more decorative, or he may have mistaken the plant; he may even have disliked the poems. One can imagine an embarrassed meeting between poet and sculptor in the Elysian Fields; the poet insists on reading the poems, while the sculptor protests that according to the *Visions of Quevedo* to hear a poet read his

2. Clare: 'Shadows of Taste'.

Helleborus niger verus.
The true blacke Hellebor.

poems is not one of the pleasures of heaven, but one of the tortures of hell.

Earlier still, even in February, we may come across in some wood, especially in the south-east of England, a more remarkable member of the family, Hellebore. Probably we have already seen in cottage gardens its near relation, Christmas Rose, astonishing us that in the depth of winter its flower should appear in a thin white dress. One might imagine it calls itself a Rose because, having a white flower, it disapproves of its proper name, Black Hellebore. The flower tends after a time to turn green, and the hanging flowers of our native Hellebores (there are two) are green. Green is an unusual colour in flowers, but being in this case a light green, like the leaves of Wood Sorrel, the plant is conspicuous across the bare brown wood. Hellebore has a great reputation. Gerard, a barber-surgeon who practised in Holborn in Shakespeare's time, calling it by different names, says it was used by husbandmen to cure cattle of pestilence, murrain and indeed any other disease:

They cut a slit or hole in the dew-lap, as they terme it (which is an emptie skin under the throat of the beast) wherein they put a piece of the root of Setterwort or Beare-foot, suffering it to remaine for certaine days together: which manner of curing they do call Settering of their cattell.

But it was as a cure, not for cattle, but for people that Hellebore was famous:

it is good for ye Epilepticall, Melancholicall, frantick, Arthriticall, Paralyticall,

says Dioscorides in Goodyer's translation. He explains how this valuable plant was dug:

When they dig it, they stand praying to Apollo and Aesculapius, observing ye Eagles flight, for they say he flies that way not without danger to them. For ye bird causeth death, if so be he see ye digging of ye Hellebore.

Above all it was good for the brain; did not Accius take it to inspire him to write another Iliad, and a certain philosopher to dispute with Zeno the Stoic? 'Drink hellebore', was a Greek's way of saying 'You are off your head'. It was a cure for every kind of madness; Horace advises anyone mad enough to have worldly ambitions to set sail for Anticyra, an island noted for its Hellebore. Whether our Hellebore can cure madness or not, a person would be mad to try so poisonous a plant; it almost killed St Martin, who ate it by mistake; the cure would be not unlike the cure, a Buttercup root, that the herbalist Parkinson recommends for toothache; by causing, as he says,

more paine than is felt by the toothach it taketh away the pain.

Winter Aconite we also find in February.

Aconitum and rash gunpowder

says Shakespeare, and though not as rash as gunpowder aconite is said to act with a fearful rapidity. De Quincey had a poor opinion of poisons, denying them a part in *Murder as One of the*

Fine Arts; but most people feel for poisons the kind of fascination they feel for snakes at the Zoo. So at one time I had a great desire to see Winter Aconite, little dreaming it grew near my home, in fact in the grounds of my neighbour, the Earl of Rosebery. Only a wall separated his property from mine, which was the public road, but it did not occur to me to look over the wall. His housekeeper used to invite me to tea, but as nothing could persuade her it was not garden flowers I was interested in but wild ones, she invited me in the time of Roses or Chrysanthemums. One February day, however, I chanced to call, and, passing through the grounds, noticed at some distance what looked like small lumps of gold in the grass. 'Goldilocks', I thought, but walking over I knew the plant could be none other than Winter Aconite. So this was the plant that had the deadly poison, this pretty plant with its yellow flower set in a whorl of leaves,

> Like tender maiden muffled from the cold,[3]

as Clare describes it. The shrieking Mandrake had to be pulled up by a dog that died of the effects –

> This Monster struck *Bellona's* self with awe,
> When first the Man-resembling Plant she saw –;[4]

the strange plant called Scythian Lamb, which grew near Samarcand, ate the grass about it till in its turn it was eaten by a wolf; Marlowe speaks of a tree called Zoacum

> With apples like the heads of damned fiends;[5]

but I felt there was something no less sinister in this small plant's seeming innocence. I spoke about it to the housekeeper at tea; I told her that two criminals had once been put to death by being given its root to eat. She grew alarmed and said she would speak to his lordship. Later I learnt that what I had seen was not the poisonous plant, its name Winter Aconite being due to a resemblance in the leaves. The true Aconite is the garden plant,

3. 'March'.
4. Cowley: *Liber Plantarum* (Latin poems translated by various hands).
5. *Tamburlaine the Great*.

occasionally wild in the West, that hides its evil nature under the mask of religion, calling itself Monkshood. It is a Buttercup too, but it blooms in summer.

If Buttercups come first in a flora, Lilies come towards the end; and indeed it seems a far cry from the one to the other. We think of Buttercups as homely plants; we almost resent that Winter Aconite, a native of Italy, should affect so much our English estates; but Lilies have been called 'the patricians of the vegetable world'. Yet they are not so grand a family after all. As originally the noble name Medici meant only apothecaries, or perhaps physicians, Lily meant only a bright flower. The plants we call Water-lilies are nearly related to the Buttercups, while the Water-lilies that Isaac Walton speaks of as chequering a meadow may have been Marsh Marigolds. The Lily of the Bible is no doubt Scarlet Anemone, a kind of Buttercup – 'his lips like lilies, dropping sweet smelling myrrh'. Daffodils are more appropriately called Lent Lilies, for they are near relations, and answer to Theophrastus's curious description of a Lily,

> a flower within a flower.

As for the members of the Lily family, some have descended lower than the apothecary's shop, serving in the kitchen as Leeks and Onions. That is indeed a downfall; was it only their sharp scent that made Borachio say,

> Alas! I'm apt to weep, though I but see
> An onion stripp'd naked?[6]

Asparagus holds an ambiguous position; in its youth it too serves in the kitchen, but later it may be promoted to the drawing-room, its green sprays of foliage setting off flowers in a vase. Yet it has received an unusual honour; some plants are called after islands, such as Candytuft, called after Candia or Crete; but Asparagus has given its name to an island off the Lizard, Asparagus Island. There it grows wild, its reptilian shoots rising in spring as though the island gave birth to serpents. Wild Garlic has too strong a breath to be admitted even to the kitchen; as Evelyn says,

6. Davenant: 'The Cruel Brother'.

Ruſcus ſiue Bruſcus.
Kneeholme, or Butchers Broome

'tis not for ladies palats, nor those who court them.[7]

Plentiful in damp woods, it tries to uphold the family reputation by having leaves like Lily of the Valley; but if anyone, mistaking it for that popular plant, picks its bursting flower-buds, it punishes his nose and fingers with a most unlily-like smell. I remember meeting its rare relation, Triangular-stalked Garlic. I came on it one April night in Cornwall, and my coming on it was literal, for I trod on the plant in stepping from a bus. Some animals, pursued by their enemies, put them off the scent, so to speak, by emitting a horrible stench. This Garlic, growing so confidently by the roadside, could not have had that intention; in any case it would have been too late. I have never known so pathetic a smell.

7. *Acetiaria.*

The Lilies might in one way be proud of Butcher's Broom, for it is the only member of the family in this country with a woody stem. A small shrub – it is sometimes called Knee-holly – it has taken to city life, perhaps not distinguishing between the dimness of a southern wood and the dingy light of a London park. Its leaves look odd, for they point up and down, but the cream-coloured flowers – we may see them in February – look odder, growing in the centre of the leaves. The oddity, however, is deceptive; the apparent leaves are flattened twigs. In Asparagus too the foliage is only apparent, the sprays being composed of numerous immature flower-stalks. So the Knee-holly is stiff and evergreen, and butchers are said to have used it to sweep their shops. On the whole the family can hardly be proud of Butcher's Broom.

What do the Lilies feel about their poor relations, the Rushes? Botanists at least take a great interest in them. Once at the Lizard I saw a woman, who paid almost no attention to two charming Lilies that grow there, Spring Squill and Chives, fling herself in ecstasy before a small Rush in a muddy puddle, crying 'Oh, the little darling'. Most people, however, disregard Rushes, thinking they scarcely have flowers, though to the botanist's eye the flowers of Rushes and Lilies bear a close resemblance. They look for signs of spring, but do not notice the pretty Wood-rush that has come out of a wood to meet them in a meadow. Rushes and Lilies are so nearly related that it is thought that at one time Rushes had larger, more Lily-like flowers, may in fact have been Lilies themselves. Dressed in gay clothes, they entertained with expensive perfumes and liquors their insect friends, painted butterflies and fur-coated bees; but prompted by some idea of economy they gave up such lavish hospitality and were content to leave the wind, without cost of carriage, to distribute their pollen. We may think it a false economy, for the flowers, no longer designed to attract, grew degenerate. 'Give and take' has been the principle guiding the evolution of flowers and insects. Sprengel, who discovered this principle, was a parson who lost his job because he took more interest in plants than in sermons; but how excellent a sermon, with floral illustrations, he might have preached on the text, 'Give and it shall be given unto you'. Indeed, this false economy seems to have reduced the Rushes to poverty, driving them from the flowery places of the earth to live huddled together, mostly in poor bogs and on barren shores. Bog Asphodel looks like a Lily that has partially fallen; it still keeps its place in the family, and no doubt deserves it, with its spike of golden flowers; yet by some botanists it has been brought down to the Rushes. Let Bog Asphodel beware!

If the Lilies are embarrassed by their poor relations, the Rushes, I confess I have been embarrassed myself. Having occasion to travel once from London to Gloucester, I studied the railway time-table and decided my best way – not the shortest, I admit – was by Bristol. I wrote to a botanist there, a friend of a friend, saying I hoped to visit him next day, early in the afternoon. Arriving at Bristol I ate a hearty lunch, and, feeling it was still too soon to call, spent half-an-hour walking up and down his street. Then I rang the bell and 'At last', he cried; 'I have been waiting lunch; you must be hungry after your journey'. A sensible person would have explained the situation, but, hating to disappoint anyone, I sat down without a word. He was one of those people who talk more than they eat, and the lunch like a wounded snake dragged its slow length along. To the physical discomfort I was suffering was added, strangely enough, a mental anxiety about my evening meal. This I had promised to have with a friend in Gloucester; but how could I see any plants and catch my train? Fortunately the plants I hoped to see grew not out in the country, as one might expect, but in Bristol itself, on the steep bank of the Avon. He showed me Rock Hutchinsia, named after an Irish botanist, Miss Hutchins, and Honewort, a cure for a swelling of the cheek called a hone. Then with the air of one who keeps the best to the last he said, 'Would you like to see something else?' 'Spring Cinquefoil?' I asked. 'Something better', he replied. 'Not Bristol Rock-cress?' I almost cried. 'Wait and see', he said with a sly smile. I followed him as he hunted about the bank. People on the promenade, leaning on the railing, watched us, some inquiring what we had lost. 'I may not find it', he said, but I somehow felt sure he would. At last he gave a cry and bent down. Hastening to the spot I found myself staring at – a Rush. With a thrill in his voice he said, 'It's Juncus –', but I could not catch the name. 'Is it really?' I said, affecting great interest. But I saw he was suspicious of my interest, and I felt embarrassed. I think he would have examined me on my attitude to Rushes, but I was saved from further awkwardness by discovering I had just time to catch my train. So thanking him I ran for a tram that stood lit up in the April dusk. He must have followed in the next tram, for as I sat in the train waiting for it to start, he appeared at the carriage window. 'I hope you are satisfied with your visit', he said. 'Delighted', I replied; 'I hardly expected to see two new plants'. 'Two? What about the Rush?' he asked sharply. 'Yes, the Rush of course', I cried, and no doubt I looked pleased, for the train was now gliding along the platform.

5   Names of Spring Flowers

'What do poets mean by hyacinthine locks?' I asked my friend, John Allan; 'do they mean blue-black hair or hair with a curled edge like a Hyacinth?' To my surprise he said 'Golden hair'. When I looked incredulous he referred me to the *Odyssey*, where Athene causes her hero's locks to flow like a hyacinth-flower, as when some skilled workman overlays gold upon silver. Zeus must have had hyacinthine locks, for sometimes they were stolen from his statues for the sake of the gold. So Timon the Misanthrope, addressing him, says,

You noble Giant-killer and Titan-conqueror, you sat still and let them crop your long locks, holding a fifteen-foot thunderbolt in your right hand.[1]

'By the way,' I asked my friend – for I remembered that at our school he had been on the side of modern languages – 'by the way, when did you learn Greek?' Tossing his head like a flower he replied, 'I can't remember now; I suppose I must always have known it'.

Classical writers had names for the plants of their own and neighbouring lands, but as it did not occur to the herbalists who tried to identify them that they might not all grow in their more northerly lands, they sometimes attached a wrong name to a plant. We can hardly think that our Leopard's-bane is the plant to which the Greeks gave so fearsome a name. The herbalist was like someone trying to identify those plants that clung about Corynna's body,

> To taste her sweetes, as Bees do swarme on them,

when Ovid saw her going to bathe:

1. Lucian.

Sacred Nepenthe, purgative of care,
And soveraine Rumex that doth rancor kill,
Sya, and Hyacinth, that Furies weare,
White and red Iessamines, Merry, Melliphill:
   Fayre Crowne-imperial, Emperor of Flowers,
Immortall Amaranth, white Aphrodill,
   And cup-like Twillpants, stroude in *Bacchus* Bowres.[2]

As for the Greek Hyacinth, we know only that like the Rose
which sprang from the blood of Adonis, and the Anemone from
Aphrodite's tears, it commemorates a hero's death, its leaves
inscribed with the words 'Alas, alas'. Whether the hero was
Hyacinthos of Sparta or Ajax of Salamis, the Greeks themselves
were uncertain:

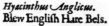

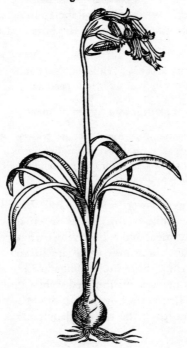

2. Chapman: 'Ovid's Banquet of Sense'.

I am a plant for which Sparta and Salamis dispute, and I mourn for either the fairest of youths or the stoutest of warriors.[3]

Clearly it was not our Hyacinth, which Linnaeus examined, and not finding it

> Like to that sanguine flower inscribed with woe,[4]

called 'non-scriptus'. So it was vain for the lovesick poet to say,

> That she might read my case
> A hyacinth I wish'd me in her hand.[5]

We have enough trouble with the names of our own plants. The flower called in Scotland Wild Hyacinth is called in England Bluebell, the name given in Scotland to Harebell, while Harebell is Shakespeare's name for Wild Hyacinth or Bluebell. What a confusion! Botanists are inclined to smile at such names, proud of their own principle, One plant, one name, and our only reply might be, Yes, but what a name! Rabelais in his excellent chapter on names of plants makes fun of the botanical name of Stitchwort:

Holosteon means all bones; whilst on the contrary there is no frailer, tenderer, nor brittler herb in the whole production of nature.

Gerard tries to explain it as a figure of speech:

In English All-bones; whereof I see no reason, except it be by the figure Antonomia; as when we say in English, He is an honest man, our meaning is that he is a knave; for this is a tender herbe having no such bony substance.

Even the gardener may scoff at the names of wild plants. Yet he too is not free from confusion, as when he calls Lilac what botanists call Syringa, and calls Syringa what they call Philadelphus. But what odd names these are in any case! Syringa is named after Syrinx, the nymph changed to a reed, or rather after the Pan's-pipes made from the reed; while Philadelphus, or, as we might say, Brotherly Love, is no doubt named after one of those kings who took the title Philadelphus or Euergetes, the

---

3. *The Greek Anthology*.
4. Milton: 'Lycidas'.
5. Drummond of Hawthornden: Madrigal.

Benefactor, sarcastically referred to in the Gospels – 'they that exercise authority are called benefactors'.

One trouble with English names is that sometimes a name is shared by two different plants. Goldilocks is a common Spring Buttercup in the South, and when a friend offered to show me Goldilocks I was surprised. Only on reflecting it was already late in August was my interest aroused. The plant he showed me was the rare Chrysocoma; it was growing near the edge of a Somerset quarry, where it may since have been blown into the air. Even two common plants may share a name, such as Lesser Celandine, a Buttercup, and Greater Celandine, a Poppy. There is a rivalry between these as to which is Pliny's Celandine, used by swallows, as he says, to restore the sight of their nestlings, even when their eyes have been picked out; but no doubt it was the Poppy. It was not, however, for the benefit of swallows that this yellow-flowering Poppy was grown in the gardens near which it is still frequently found. Poppies exude from their broken stem a kind of milk; possibly the Latin name Papaver, from which Poppy is derived, is connected with the word pap. As Greater Celandine's milk is yellow, it was considered a cure for jaundice, a homoeo-pathic cure, we may say, for homoeopathy means sympathy, the sympathy in this case being shown in the likeness of the milk's colour to the patient's. Perhaps it was a homoeopathic cure in the other sense, taken in small doses, for it is a bitter milk. Or did people use it only externally? John Wesley, who wrote a book, *Primitive Physick*, recommends the plant, but advises people to put its leaves in their shoes. Lesser Celandine was also a medicinal plant, but all the medicine these plants give us now, and indeed it is the meaning of the name Celandine or Swallow-wort, is the good news that that 'flying Almanack', the swallow, has arrived. That the Dead Nettles, White and Red, should share a name with Stinging Nettle is not so strange. Their leaves are somewhat alike; it is even thought that by this likeness Dead Nettles gain protection from grazing animals, who mistake them for Stinging Nettles. Perhaps animals would not make such a mistake; I can scarcely believe a cow is as ignorant of botany as myself, for sent by my wife into the garden to pick Mint, I brought back, as she pointed out, not only Mint but leaves of Dead Nettle. Several plants have leaves much alike, usually aromatic, pleasant to us, but probably distasteful to animals. Let us hope Ophelia did not make a mistake, and they were stingless Dead Nettles she wove in her fantastic garlands

> Of crow-flowers, nettles, daisies and long purples.

It is commoner for a plant to have several names. Yellow Dead Nettle, that in spring hedges dons its golden helmets – do they not protect the pollen? – has two other names, Archangel and Weasel-snout. Such strangely diverse names suggest a fallen archangel, changed to a demon; but Weasel-snout is only the name given by the profane to a plant that like Angelica and its garden relation, Archangelica, drove away diseases and evil spirits. We should not be surprised at so exalted a name as Archangel, for a Latin poet, before venturing to gather herbs, addresses them:

> With all you potent herbs do I now intercede, and to your majesty make my appeal. For this in suppliant wise I implore and plead, that I may be allowed to gather you, with the favour of your majesty.[6]

How differently today do people pick wild flowers! Wood Sorrel also has two such different names as Stubwort and Alleluia. Stubwort, however, is a pretty name, due to the plant's pleasant habit of growing on mossy stubs; while the other is a foolish name if it be true, as Parkinson says,

> it is called by Apothecaries in their shoppes *Alleluia*, because about that time it is in flower, when Alleluja in ancient times was wont to be sung in the churches

– between Easter and Whitsuntide. But possibly Parkinson was wrong; the plant may have been so named because its threefold leaf was thought to illustrate the Holy Trinity. Blooming about St Patrick's Day, it has often been identified with the plant the saint is said to have used for that purpose, now commonly called Shamrock.

A curious thing is that many favourite flowers, such as the Rose, are known by a foreign name. No doubt they had an English name once – the Rose was called Hip-bramble – but as

6. *Precatio Omnium Herbarum* (unknown author).

people today, despising available English names, call their garden
plants by botanical ones

> That would have made Quintilian stare and gasp,[7]

so our forefathers affected the Latin names used by the monks.
In the Prayer Book we keep Latin and English words side by
side, though their meaning is the same – 'confirm and strengthen
us in all goodness' – but many English plant-names have
disappeared. Fortunately the Latin names on the whole are
pleasant; Comfrey, which seems to mean a plant that heals,
sounds no worse than Yalluc, and Mercury, derived from the
Roman god, is as dignified as Cheadle. We cannot complain we
speak of White Violets instead of Boneworts. Sometimes we
degrade a classical name by the addition of Dog.

> We call by the name of a dog a hound, a fish and a star,

says Seneca,[8] but we have done worse, having given the name to
several plants. Dog's Mercury is so called only because it has not
the medicinal property of its relation, Annual Mercury, and Dog
Violet because it is scentless. Dog Rose is more pardonable, for
it is the translation of a Greek name that means a cure for
hydrophobia. Pliny tells of a woman who, admonished by a
vision in her sleep, sent her son a decoction of Wild Rose root,
curing him of a dog-bite. Sometimes, however, a classical name
is obscure; why a small pinkish flower should be called Fumitory,
Earth-smoke, is no clearer than the smoke itself; and why should
a large Maple be called Sycamore, which means Fig-mulberry?
On the other hand anyone can see in a bunch of Columbines a
group of conferring doves. Or a classical name may be mislead-
ing; a Primrose is not a kind of Rose. But who can say that a
Daffodil, our wild Narcissus, belies the derivation of its name
and is not the Asphodel of the Elysian Fields?

> . . . the narcissus that fed by heavenly dew blooms morn by morn
> with fair clusters, crown of the Great Goddesses from of old.[9]

Some, not content with monkish Latin, also affected the

7. Milton: Sonnet.
8. *On Benefits*.
9. Sophocles: *Oedipus at Colonus*.

French names of the Normans. Daffodil came from Asphodel through the French. The variegated Violas that grow in cornfields and hill pastures are called Pansies, from the French *pensée*. 'There is pansies, that's for thoughts', says Ophelia, speaking no doubt of the garden flower, and Cornelio, more precise, says,

> Oh, that's for lovers' thoughts.[10]

Evidently sad thoughts, for it is the little western flower that was struck by Cupid's bolt,

> Before milk-white, now purple with love's wound,
> And maidens call it love-in-idleness,[11]

that is, love in vain. How different is the English name, Heartsease. If Heartsease does not mean a heart stimulant, it suggests at least a cheerful plant:

> Thyme for truth, rosemary for remembrance, roses for love, heartsease for you,

says the Gardener in Campion's *Entertainment*, and Bunyan's Shepherd's Boy

> wears more of the herb called heart's ease in his bosom, than he that is clad in silk and velvet.

Dandelion is French for Lion's Tooth, the name referring to the lobed leaves. One might have thought it would be named from the flower, the golden flower that, followed by its grey seed-head, inspired Hurdis to a remarkable flight of imagination:

> Dandelion this,
> A college youth that flashes for a day
> All gold; anon he doffs his gaudy suit,
> Touch'd by the magic hand of some grave Bishop,
> And all at once, by commutation strange,
> Becomes a Reverend Divine.[12]

Hurdis was made Professor of Poetry at Oxford!

Most wild flowers, however, have plain English names; yet

10. Chapman: 'All Fools'.
11. *A Midsummer Night's Dream*.
12. 'The Village Curate'.

their meaning is not always plain. The name Veronica, or True Image, compares the flower to St Veronica's cloth, 'portrayed with His blessed Face, who is the flower of the earth'; but what does the English name, Speedwell, mean? To the idea that it means Good-bye – the petals soon fall when it is picked – we may bid Good-bye. Another curious explanation is that people used the plant to hasten or ease a journey. They so used Mugwort:

. . . and if a Footman takes *Mugwort* and puts it in his Shoos in the Morning, he may go forty Miles before Noon and not be weary,

says Coles. But no one seems to have tried the experiment with Speedwell. If Speed means prosper, as in 'Speed the plough', perhaps the name means Good-luck. But in some cases it is well the meaning is not plain. If Speedwell is a pleasant name, there are plants, common ones too,

> That liberal shepherds give a grosser name.[13]

Yet those who gave them vulgar names may in other ways have been wiser than ourselves,

who cast a more careless Eye on these common Hieroglyphicks, and disdain to such Divinity from the flowers.[14]

Plants told them many things about the Virgin Mary not recorded in the Bible: Lady's-smock that she laid out her lilac-coloured dress on spring meadows; Lady's-mantle that she wore a greenish cloak; Lady's Bedstraw that her coverlet was yellow; Lady's-fingers that she had long tapering hands, and Lady's-tresses that she wore her hair in plaits. Why does one of our rarest Orchids survive in the North, but to tell us that her slippers were purple and gold?

13. *Hamlet.*
14. Sir Thomas Browne: *Religio Medici.*

6   A Simple Method

When I brought home my first wild flower and found someone to identify it as Speedwell, I was in the position of one who knows that a certain animal is a dog, but whether bulldog, Alsatian or pug, has no idea. Even early in spring there are three common Speedwells, Buxbaum's, Grey and Ivy-leaved, drowsy plants that scarcely open their blue eyes to the sun. But if I had not gone far in my study of wild flowers, I had at least hit on a good method.

'Oh! that we had a book of botany', exclaims Dorothy Wordsworth in her *Journal*. Perhaps her brother William refused to let her have one, a botanist being to him

> a fingering slave,
> One that would peep and botanize
> Upon his mother's grave.[1]

But he might have been the better for such a book himself; he might not then have spoken of

> Butter that had imbibed from meadow-flowers
> A golden hue,[2]

as though cows ate Buttercups. Buttercups are more or less poisonous, though fortunately the poison disappears in the making of hay. But probably it was not a book of botany Dorothy wanted, but one of those books, common today, that offer a simple method of identifying wild flowers. I have tried such books myself, but found that if they were simple, I was simpler still. It was not that I did badly with them, but rather that I did too well; I kept finding rare plants in places where they

1. 'A Poet's Epitaph'.
2. 'The Excursion'.

never grew, and even plants that apparently no one had discovered but myself. So I fell back on the method I had adopted with the Speedwell, the simple method of asking someone who knew. People like to give information. If a car draws up beside me and the driver inquires his way to a place, I get so excited that the chances are I direct him wrongly. During army manoeuvres I so misdirected a stream of lorries that I had to remain indoors for the rest of the day in case they should return by my village. But a botanist on being handed a wild flower is not likely to lose his head; and why deprive him of the pleasure of telling its name? My method is so simple that I am surprised no 'book of botany' recommends it. But if simple, it is also philosophic. 'About equestrian matters should we not have recourse to horsemen?' asks Socrates. 'Yes', replies Alcibiades. 'And about naval matters to sailors?' and again the answer is 'Yes'. Might not my method be called the Socratic?

For a person like myself to attempt to identify wild flowers is mere madness; and in June and July, when they are numerous, it would be midsummer madness. The difficulties are almost unimaginable. A plant may deceive us by its name, even its botanical name. If it is called montana or mountain, or something of the kind, the chances are it grows in a lowland valley. Veronica montana, Mountain Speedwell, is scarce in Scotland, but common in moist woods in the South; Epilobium montanum, Mountain Willow-herb, is a garden weed, though I admit it often gets as far as climbing a wall: Geranium pyrenaicum, Mountain Cranesbill, grows in meadows, while Anemone apennina, Blue Mountain Anemone, I have seen only at Mitcham. I suppose mountains have grown in size since Christian in the *Pilgrim's Progress* saw 'a wide field, full of dark mountains', where Hypocrisy stumbled and fell. Or a name may deceive us in another way. Year after year I searched the autumn stubbles for Adonis autumnalis; Venus could not have searched more patiently. At last a botanist told me where I could find it, a field near Old Sarum. Hoping that autumnalis did not necessarily mean September, I risked going there in August. Failing to find the plant, 'I suppose I was too soon', I wrote to my friend. 'Yes, by about ten months', he replied; 'it blooms in June'. Now botanists in a shamefaced way are calling it Adonis annua.

Polygala flore cæruleo.
Blew Milke woort.

Darwin said that bees were good botanists, meaning that they could distinguish a flower under varying colours; some of us who, lacking the bees' intelligence, are not botanists, may be deceived by a colour. Though I have never mistaken Milkwort, its colour may have deceived wet nurses. Reading in Gerard's *Herbal*, at one time the medical book of a country house, that the plant was so named from its

> virtues in procuring milk in the breasts of nurses,

they may have gone seeking it, guided by his description:

> The floures grow at the top, of a blew color, fashioned like a little bird, with wings, taile, and bodie, easie to be discerned by them that doe observe the same.

Yet they may have been misled, for while the description is no doubt accurate, it does not refer to the plant's remarkable patriotism in producing a flower that may be red or white or blue. But a more likely difficulty arises from different plants resembling one another; this occurs particularly among those yellow-flowering plants that have Hawk in their name. How happy is the countryman who calls them all Dandelion, compared with a botanist I knew who, cursing Hawkweeds and Hawkbits, cried, 'A plague on both your houses'. These plants are called Hawk because hawks are said to have used them to sharpen their sight; perhaps they sharpened it by learning to distinguish the various kinds. I cannot claim to have the eyesight of a hawk.

But someone may say, 'Surely all these difficulties could be overcome by even an elementary knowledge of botany?' No doubt they could; in fact such a knowledge is implied in my Simple Method, not of course one's own knowledge, but the botanist's. Some people do not desire a knowledge of botany:

> Quid curae nobis de generibus et speciebus?

they might say with Thomas à Kempis. They doubt if they could feel the ravishments and ecstasies felt by Rousseau:

> Rien n'est plus singulier que les ravissemens, les extases que j'éprouvois à chaque observation que je faisois sur la structure et l'organisation végétale.[3]

They may be horrified to think how, in identifying a flower,

> A monster with a glass
> Computes the stamens in a breath,
> And has her in a class;[4]

they would not like to be such a monster. They may feel that botany is irrelevant to their particular interest in plants; they may even say, with a side glance at the botanist,

> But nature is a stranger yet;
>   The ones that cite her most
> Have never passed her haunted house,
>   Nor simplified her ghost.[5]

3. *Rêveries du Promeneur Solitaire.*
4. Emily Dickinson.
5. Emily Dickinson.

The chief reason, however, why a person like myself should not attempt to identify wild flowers is the moral danger. If there is any dishonesty in our nature, sooner or later wild flowers will bring it out. Even to express an opinion may be dangerous; it was through yielding to the temptation that I fell into the sin of Balaam. One spring I was invited by a lady, a stranger, to come and see Perfoliate Pennycress. Though I knew it was considered a Gloucestershire plant, and she lived in Somerset, I accepted the invitation. We were to meet in a certain town, at an appointed place. My train made me late, but, as it turned out, I was much too early. I looked expectantly at each woman who approached, but only to receive a cold, hostile stare. To a lover of wild flowers of course that kind of thing is all in the day's work. At last she arrived in a car, and when she had identified me, we drove out into the country. 'I am anxious to have your opinion of the plant', she said, 'so we will look at it first and then have tea'. Delightful arrangement, I thought; but when the car stopped outside her house, I imagined she had changed her mind. But no, for 'Well, do you see it?' she asked. I did indeed, Perfoliate Pennycress without a doubt; but I also saw where it was growing, on the outer bank of her garden. 'I know it is supposed to grow only in Gloucestershire', she said, 'but I am sure none of my predecessors could have planted it. Do you think it is wild?' I avoided answering the question; but afterwards, as I sat at tea in her charming house, eating bread and her own honey, reflecting too on the long journey I had taken to see the plant, I expressed the opinion that it was wild. 'I am so glad you think so', she said, as though I were a final authority. An hour or two later, however, as I again sat at tea, this time in a railway refreshment-room, my conscience began to talk. 'Well, a fine fool you have made of yourself today; you came to Somerset for what you knew was a Gloucestershire plant'. 'But it is just possible –', I began. 'Don't argue', continued my conscience; 'you know your weakness; you are too willing to believe what you want to believe. Your first thought was that the plant was not wild. Remember what Bishop Butler says in his sermon on Balaam; first thoughts are best in matters of conscience. Do you want to be a Balaam?' I recognized the truth of what my conscience said; I had long known how wild flowers tempt us to be dishonest, to believe we have identified a plant when we are not sure, or, as in this case, to regard as wild what may be a garden escape. Returning in the train that evening I felt miserable; in fact I did not cheer up till a week later, when a botanist assured me that the plant I had seen was genuinely wild.

7   Spring Herbs

When Edward Thomas went to live near Epping Forest, he was distressed to find it so bare of the spring flowers he expected. If people had always had the deadly affection for wild flowers they now have, we might wonder in what numbers even Primroses and Bluebells would be left. But formerly people did not much regard them for their own sakes, or gather them to any wasteful extent. Who would want to pick a flower he called a Cowslop? If the list of wild flowers in *Britannia's Pastorals* suggests that people always liked them, the list in *Poly-Olbion* suggests that they looked at them with a utilitarian eye. They thought, not so much of wild flowers, as of herbs, which they might gather or transplant for some useful purpose. The word arbour was herber till it got mixed up with the Latin word arbor. Shenstone's Schoolmistress scorned flowers of any kind in her garden:

> Where no vain flow'r disclos'd a gaudy streak,
> But herbs for use, and physick, not a few.

Many names suggest that people were less interested in a plant's appearance than in its taste. Hairy Bittercress they would leave to grow on the roadside or mossy wall. Wood Sorrel, Sheep's-sorrel and Sorrel-dock all share a name that means sour. Wood Sorrel was also called Alleluia, but that did not prevent its being used in salads; Sheep's-sorrel, like Lamb's-lettuce, may have been thought fit only for sheep, but Sorrel-dock was eaten along with mutton. The name Garlic Mustard, while not such a mouthful as Worm-seed Treacle-mustard, suggests enough condiment to explain the plant's other name, Sauce-alone. Field Pepperwort may not have been used itself, but its rare summer relative, Broad-leaved Pepperwort, also called Dittander, was used before pepper became common. Winter-cress has the botanical name Barbarea,

Raphanus sylveſtris officinarum, lepidium Aegineta
Dittander,and Pepperwoort.   (*L'Obelis.*

probably because its leaves were sought as early as St Barbara's feast-day, which falls in December.

People of course were not 'blind mouths', and some of these plants have pleasanter names; Winter-cress and Garlic Mustard, two upright plants, are also called Yellow Rocket and Jack-by-the-hedge. Yet even the names that suggest a plant's use may have a charm, like old utensils that have almost become things of beauty. Any name is better than Field Pepperwort's botanical name, Lepidium Smithii, Smith's Scaly Plant. Ruskin in one of his bad-tempered moods says that plants are named, some from diseases, some from vermin, some from blockheads and the rest anyhow; by blockheads he means botanists. Yet botanists may be allowed to lend their names to a few plants, when so many plants have lent us names, some appropriate enough, such as Coles and Culpeper for those two famous herbalists.

A flower called Treacle is fortunate in having a name with so rich a history. Derived from the Greek word for a wild beast, Treacle was first an antidote against snake-bite; then it became the name of various compounds, cures for poisoning and plague. Celsus gives thirty-six ingredients for his Treacle, including Poppytears, Myrrh, Opopanax, Opobalsamum, Gentian, Saffron and Shepherd's-purse, pounded and taken up in honey. Venice Treacle, reputed the best, had sixty-one ingredients. Evelyn saw it being prepared at Venice,

the making and extraordinary ceremonie whereof I had been curious to observe, for 'tis extremely pompous and worth seeing.[1]

The name came to be applied to any medicine; where we read, 'Is there no balm in Gilead?' Coverdale's Bible has 'There is no more Triacle in Galaad'. But originally it was such a mithridate as Mithridates, King of Pontus, took to make himself immune from poison:

> And easy, smiling, seasoned sound,
> Sate the king when healths went round.
> They put arsenic in his meat
> And stared aghast to watch him eat;
> They poured strychnine in his cup
> And shook to see him drink it up.[2]

Plants were regarded more as medicine than food. The most widely read botanical book, translated into such different languages as Hebrew and Anglo-Saxon, was written by a surgeon in Nero's army, Dioscorides, and called *De Materia Medica*; Gerard's *Herbal*, also written by a surgeon of sorts, had a great popularity, not for its botanical information fortunately, but for its medical advice. Was it not said, 'The Lord created medicines out of the earth; And a prudent man will have no disgust at them'? The word physician means literally a naturalist. But with so many precious herbs at hand people hardly needed a doctor – was there not a plant called All-heal? – or even a surgeon – was its other name not Carpenter-grass? –

1. *Diary*.
2. A. E. Housman: 'A Shropshire Lad'.

Gramen Leucanthemum.
Stitchwoort.

for every man
Was his own patient and physician.[3]

So to Ruskin's disgust many plants are named after diseases. Certainly that beautiful plant called by botanists Stellaria, because its flower shines like a clear white light, deserved a better name than Stitchwort, and Whitlow-grass, which, liking the loose soil of a mole-hill, makes it a heap of silver, deserved better than to be called after an inflammation of the finger-nail. Coltsfoot on Tweed-side is called Tussilago, which might be translated Cough-mixture. (Is this botanical name a sign of high education of Tweed-side? Yet a South American plant, Galinsoga, that came as seed with imported wool, was called first Gallant Soldier and then Soldier of the Queen.) Golden Saxifrage may seem strangely

3. Browne: 'Britannia's Pastorals'.

named, as it grows, not among rocks, but in soft damp places, making a Pactolus of a woodland rill; but Saxifrages or Stone-breakers get their name from a different kind of stone they break:

> Saxifrage is good, and Hart's-tongue for the stone.[4]

Spurge, on the other hand, may have been applied only externally, expurgating warts, for the milk that flows from its broken stem has a fiery and frightening bitterness on the tongue. When Rossetti's eyes fell on Wood Spurge, did he recognize a correspondence between the bitterness of the plant and his own bitter grief?

> Between my knees my forehead was, –
> My lips, drawn in, said not Alas!
> My hair was over in the grass,
> My naked ears heard the day pass.[5]

Plants then were simples, by which was meant a simple medicine as opposed to a compound. So Jaques in a figure of speech describes his melancholy as

> compounded of many simples, extracted from many objects.

As each illness had a herb to cure it, simples were to be preferred to compounds. King James I had a poor opinion of doctors for using compounds:

> The art of phisitians is very imperfect, for I doubt not but for every disease there is in nature a severall symple, if they could find it out, so that their compounds do rather show their ignorance than knowledge.[6]

Thomas Fuller, so far from thinking that to have faith in simples is to be simple-minded, says:

> England especially, affordeth excellent plants: were it not partly for men's laziness, that they will not seek them; partly for their ignorance, that they know not when they have found them; and partly for their pride and peevishness, because, when found, they disdain to use and apply them.[7]

4. Drayton: *Poly-Olbion*.
5. 'The Woodspurge'.
6. Overbury: *Crumms Fal'n from King James's Table*.
7. *Worthies of England*.

George Herbert thinks that the Country Parson's job is not only a cure of souls but also a cure of bodies:

Accordingly, for salves, his wife seeks not the city, but prefers her garden and fields before all outlandish gums.

In fact, as the two things are not so different,

in curing of any, the Parson and his Family use to premise prayers, for this is to cure like a Parson, and this raiseth the action from the Shop, to the Church.[8]

But no doubt many people would prefer the shop. Drug is said to mean dried plant, and more than twenty of our native plants have the specific name, officinalis, which means they were sold in shops. Others, believing that

by some signature
Nature herself doth point us out a cure,[9]

would gather their own simples. In *Poly-Olbion* Hampstead boasts

in simples to have skill,
And therefore by desert to be the noblest Hill.

That the shop was sometimes neglected may account for the phrase 'a drug on the market'. Some herbs would seem to come at the right time; Bishop Wilson notes in his *Diary*

a very sickly spring stitch,

and, sure enough, Stitchwort blooms in spring. But people must have thought it a singular providence that plants flourished most in summer, while illness was more prevalent in winter. But they were provident themselves, cutting and drying their plants before autumn. Is that why we speak of a scheme as 'cut and dried'?

That plants themselves indicated in some way their use was a belief expressed in the famous Doctrine of Signatures. Coles was an exponent of this doctrine.

Though Sin and Sathan have plunged mankinde into an Ocean of Infirmities (for before the Fall Man was not subject to Diseases) yet the

8. *The Countrey Parson.*
9. Browne: 'Britannia's Pastorals'.

mercy of God which is over all his Workes, maketh Grasse to grow upon the Mountaines, and Herbes for the use of Men, and hath not onely stamped upon them (as upon every Man) a distinct forme, but also given them particular Signatures, whereby a Man may read, even in legible Characters, the use of them.

A Walnut, having a hard shell like a skull and a kernel configured like a brain, signified that it was a cure for all troubles of the head. Perhaps it would be fanciful to suppose that a trouble of the head caused Walnuts to be associated with wine, or for that matter with the nectar of the gods – the Latin name for Walnut is Juglans or Jove's Nut. Yet a plant's signature might not always be clear, any clearer than our own. What is there about Maidenhair Fern to suggest a cure for baldness? One would have thought Skullcap better, but that was a cure for insomnia. So the discovery of a plant's virtue was sometimes attributed to a famous person, such as Solomon, who, as the Scripture says, 'spake of trees, from the cedar which is in Lebanon even unto the hyssop that springeth out of the wall', and, as Josephus adds,

described them all like a philosopher, and demonstrated his exquisite knowledge of their several properties.[10]

Yet it is still not clear whether the power of Solomon's Seal to seal up wounds is indicated by its flowers, hanging like seals, or by seal-like scars on the underground stem. The god Mercury was supposed to have discovered the virtue of the plant Mercury. Here the signature seemed obvious enough, for this plant, like ourselves, was created in two forms, male and female. People believed that if they ate the male plant their next child would be a boy; unfortunately they mistook the sexes and ate the female plant.

Plants of course had other uses. Ground-ivy was called Alehoof, or Ale-ivy, because it was used in making ale. A rushlight was made of the pith of Rushes, and Gold of Pleasure provided oil. But their main use was medicinal. It is the medicinal use of Tobacco that Burton praises in *The Anatomy of Melancholy*:

Tobacco, divine, rare, superexcellent tobacco, which goes far beyond all the panaceas, potable gold, and philosopher's stones, a sovereign

10. *Antiquities of the Jews.*

remedy in all diseases. A good vomit, I confess, a vertuous herb, if it be well qualified, opportunely taken, and medicinally used; but as it is commonly abused by most men, which take it as tinkers do ale, 'tis a plague, a mischief, a violent purger of goods, lands, health, hellish, devilish and damned tobacco, the ruine and overthrow of body and soul.

Other plants he praises too; yet after all he has to confess,

> A new physician needs a new churchyard.

In the *Visions of Quevedo*, when a notable murderer arrives in hell, he is sent among the doctors. To hear them call over their simples, the Spaniard says,

would make you swear they were raising so many devils. There's your opopanax, buphthalmus, astaphylinos, alectorolophos, ophioscorodon, anemosphorus, etc. And by all this formidable bombast, is meant nothing in the world but a few paltry roots, as carrots, turnip, skirrets, radish and the like.

Even Dr John Hill, though he regarded

a CULPEPPER as a more respectable person than a LINNAEUS or a DILLENIUS,

and indeed botanists but

> as the seconds in this science,

showed some shrewdness in his remark,

He who seeks the herb for its cure, will find it half effected by the walk.

We can believe it as we watch the water-drinkers at Harrogate, encouraged by the band, walking down to the Pump Room in the early morning. It may not be altogether a gain that people have forsaken the fields and hedges for the chemist's shop, where brightly-coloured bottles put the flowers to shame.

What, one may ask, can the plants themselves think, those neglected herbs,

> Whose virtues only in them died,
> As rural life gave way to pride?[11]

Not even a Costard with a broken shin now cries,

11. Clare: 'Cowper Green'.

O, sir, plantain, a plain plantain! no salve, sir, but a plantain!

Yet Plantain was once considered such a healer that put in a pot where bits of meat are boiling, it makes them into a steak. Self-heal no longer invites us with 'Physician, heal thyself'. Is Rupture-wort so rare a plant because it has gone out of practice? Robert Frost, imagining that the tombstones of a disused graveyard must wonder why people no longer come to be buried, says,

> It would be easy to be clever
> And tell the stones: Men hate to die
> And have stopped dying now forever.
> I think they would believe the lie. [12]

Perhaps the herbs, left to grow in the fields, imagine that people are no longer ill. So the Oaks, planted in Nelson's time to build a new navy, may now suppose that wars have ceased in all the world.

But if people do not gather simples like Romeo's friend the Friar, they still walk in the country and pick wild flowers. This may seem an even more foolish occupation; no doubt their tinctures, juleps, boluses and electuaries did people some good, but what is gained by picking wild flowers? Keats, when he speaks of the beauty of Daffodils, adds, 'with the green world they live in'; and wild flowers without that are poor things compared with garden flowers, and when brought into a house, pathetic as a song-bird in a cage. They cease to be themselves; in fact we can no more bring wild flowers into a house than we can bring a rainbow. And Primroses and Bluebells may in time become scarce, and all England an Epping Forest. Anne Pratt spoke of Daphne Mezereon as common; now it is one of the rarest plants, its whereabouts always a closely guarded secret. When a friend took me to see it in a wood, climbing the wall he laid his finger on his lips to enjoin silence; yet there could have been no human being within miles. This particular shrub people have not so much picked as transplanted to their gardens; perhaps I should say transported, a cottage garden being a kind of Botany Bay. As a botanist Sir Joseph Banks could be excused for collecting the plants he laid out to dry on that Australian beach;

12. 'In a Disused Graveyard'.

but there is no excuse for ravishing Daphne Mezereon from its native woods. The nymph Daphne eluded the grasp of Apollo by changing to a plant, but being a plant already has brought no safety to this Daphne. Perhaps too, we do wrong to destroy creatures who, for all we know, may enjoy the air they breathe. Even a Potato, when it is peeled, breathes more quickly; in fact, for a Potato it may be said to pant. Whether this habit of picking wild flowers is justified or not, I can argue only from my own experience.

Till near the middle of the eighteenth century Fritillary as a native plant appears to have been unnoticed by botanists; now everyone has heard of it, even though they cannot pronounce its name or scan Matthew Arnold's line,

I know what white, what purple fritillaries.[13]

Walking one day through a Berkshire town I noticed from the corner of my eye a bunch of Fritillaries on a window-ledge. Knocking at the door I asked the woman where she had found the flowers. She entertained me with a long story about her son who set off on his cycle each Sunday to court a young woman in a distant village, and who the Sunday before had brought them home. I thanked her, and with the name of the village in my mind turned away. Though there was no hope of my walking so far that afternoon, my steps instinctively moved in the direction, and when a man, driving a car; stopped to ask where I was going, the name of the village leapt to my lips. 'Jump in', he said and, when I was seated, 'Going to call on the Duke of Wellington?' he asked. The question surprised me, but, supposing he meant some inn of that name in the village, I replied, 'That's right'. For a moment he looked at me queerly; then, as though dismissing something from his mind, he suggested, 'You are after the snake's head?' This question seemed more mysterious than the first, but pondering over it I remembered that Snake's-head was another name for Fritillary, and I said 'That's right'. When we came in sight of a large mansion with a flag flying, I understood why the name of the village, Stratfield Saye, had been vaguely familiar, and understood too the jocoseness of his question about the Duke of Wellington. He dropped me at a field-gate where a woman sat

13. 'Thyrsis.'

collecting money. Paying my pence I entered the field, maroon-coloured with the drooping heads of Fritillaries. People moved slowly about, stooping to pick those flowers that looked like repentant serpents. All was so unexpected and strange that I had the feeling I was in heaven; I was even troubled to think that I was not engaged like the others. Picking flowers seemed the only occupation in heaven. But if in heaven, why not on earth? Perhaps something can be said for picking wild flowers.

8 Trees and Shrubs in May

Latimer says in one of his Sermons that having arranged to preach in a certain town, he arrived expecting to find a large congregation but found instead the church door locked.

I tarried there halfe an houer and more, at last the keye was founde, and one of the parishe commes to me and sayes. Syr thys is a busye daye wyth us, we can not heare you, it is Robyn hoodes daye. The parishe are gone a brode to gather for Robyn hoode . . . It is no laughynge matter my friends, it is a wepynge matter, a heavy matter, a heavy matter, under the pretence for gatherynge for Robyn hoode, a traytoure and a thefe, to put out a preacher, to have hys office lesse estemed, to prefer Robyn hod before the ministracion of Gods word.

To gather for Robin Hood, to go out on May morning and bring home Hawthorn blossom and other flowers to the sound of horn and tabor, to decorate and dance round a may-pole, was a great ceremony. Even a London church, St Andrew Undershaft, gets its name from a may-pole that overtopped its steeple. Yet nowadays, if we walk in the country on May morning, we might wonder about the reason. Was it that people felt the trees and flowers had come to life again?

> And yet how still the landscape stands,
>   How nonchalant the wood,
> As if the resurrection
>   Were nothing very odd.[1]

Or if the landscape is not still, nor the wood nonchalant, it is because they are agitated by a cold wind that makes us sympathize with Herrick's Corinna, who lay so late abed that morning; a wind that drives home the proverb,

1. Emily Dickinson.

> Cast not a clout
> Till may be out.

Very likely the Hawthorn blossom is not out, though it is called May after the month of May. The explanation of this lies in a change, not in the climate, but in the calendar, May now starting almost a fortnight earlier than it did when Milton wrote his 'Ode on May Morning'.

But in spite of horns and tabors, people seem to have been half afraid of Hawthorn blossom; they were careful not to carry it into their houses, but left it outside, on the door and windows,

> each street a Parke
> Made green, and trimm'd with trees.[2]

Cerasus vulgaris.
The common Englifh Cherrie tree.

2. Herrick: 'Corinna's going a Maying'.

Perhaps Walter de la Mare suggests the reason when he quotes, 'The hawthorn hath a deathly smell'. A Hawthorn hedge is called a quick to distinguish it from a fence of dead wood, but its blossom has a warm heavy scent that reminds some people of a death chamber. For long it was a common belief that it kept the smell of the Great Plague of London. Botanists say it contains a substance, trimethylamine, which is also found in decaying fish. It is pleasant to the eyes, a snow in May that mocks the winter snow; it is because the days are growing warmer that a Hawthorn hedge

> Bursts her full bodice, and reveals
> Her fair white body in the light;[3]

but to some people it is not an altogether cheerful tree.

The Cherry used to be called the Merry. Merry is a false singular from the French Merise (Wild Cherry), as Cherry is from Cerise; but before I knew better I thought it was the adjective merry, meaning pleasant, as in 'merry England' and 'the merry month of May'. Certainly no tree in May looks merrier than the tall Gean of the woods or the Dwarf Cherry of the hedges. Even the northern Bird Cherry, though its fruits may be fit only for birds, has rich clusters of flowers, not unlike a White Laburnum; indeed it must have wondered, if it overheard the conversation, why Coleridge wanted to plant Laburnums in the woods about Grasmere.[4] The fruits of wild Cherries are of small account – it is the Gean, not the Bird Cherry, that botanists call Prunus avium – at least of small account now that they have given us the Dukes, Morellos and Bigaroons of our orchards. The leaves, however, are a different matter; 'Loveliest of trees, the cherry now' might as well be said in autumn as in spring. It is not our yellow-leaved Maple that in autumn 'burns itself away' – had Tennyson been reading of the Canadian Maple? – but the wild Cherry. White as the Angel of the Annunciation in May, in autumn it is like Manoah's angel, who departed in a flame of fire.

By May Blackthorn and Bullace have lost their flowers:

> Like the fam'd Semele, they die away
> In the Embraces of the God of Day.[5]

3. W. H. Davies: 'When Leaves Begin'.
4. Dorothy Wordsworth: *Journals*.
5. Cowley: *Liber Plantarum*.

We shall scarcely notice these shrubs again till they show their blue or yellow Plums. Ezekiel was a true prophet when he denied that because the fathers had eaten sour grapes the children's teeth must be set on edge; from these wild Plums, harsh to our fore-fathers, have come Damsons and Greengages. But May is the month when Wild Pear and Apple attract attention, so covered with blossom that they look like fallen clouds. In *The Greek Anthology* a Pear, brought from the woods into an orchard, says,

Gardener, I am deeply grateful for thy pains; it is owing to thee that I am now enrolled in the noble tribe of fruit-trees;

but the Pears that grow wild in our woods and hedges appear to have escaped from cultivation, no doubt as ignorant seeds, ungrateful for the gardener's kindness to their parents. The Pear's blossom is pure white, as though it scorned the superstition that a wedding is unlucky in May; the Apple's is more bashful,

Outside a blush and inside snow,[6]

like Coventry Patmore's Angel in the House. Orchard Apples, as we know, show great delicacy about marrying their immediate relations. Tables in old churches forbid us to marry our uncles and aunts, grandfathers and grandmothers, common practices with plants; most orchard Apples, even more careful, will not mingle with their kind, and the gardener mixes his Cox's Orange Pippins and Blenheim Oranges with other varieties of tree. But what fruits they bear, and how productive are some of these in their turn,

apples, from whose womb
Barrels of lusty cider come![7]

But the great glory of an English May is Gorse or Furze. Growing best in our temperate climate, for it is not the hardy shrub it looks, it might give us our national flower. Pod-bearing plants, such as Peas, Beans and Clover, enrich the soil, as Virgil knew; for the same reason – they fix nitrogen from the under-ground air – they can grow in poor places. So Gorse covers barren, wind-dried hills, though it replaces with spines its more

6. Coventry Patmore: 'The Victories of Love'.
7. W. H. Davies: 'Let Me Confess'.

natural leaves, the trefoil leaves it bore as a seedling, to preserve its moisture. Broom, its relation and rival in the North, fares better perhaps; yet its leaves are small and often soon dropped, the green stems, ridged to provide a larger surface, carrying on their work. If it has no spines like Gorse to protect it from browsing animals, it has a bitter juice, almost the only pod-bearing plant that is poisonous. It is surprising that these plants, so impoverished in their leaves, should make such a floral display. It is of 'the bonnie broom' that Border ballads speak, though it was not too bonnie to be used as the brush which now, mostly made of Hazel-twigs, is still called a broom. But I prefer the Gorse, if only because I dyed my Easter eggs with its yellow flowers. Before I ate them I had to roll them down a slope till the shells broke, for that was the ritual. The scent of Gorse, or Whin as I called it then, brings it back, though it is a long time since I killed the goose that laid those golden eggs.

But trees and shrubs are to be praised not only for their flowers. We may admire the Rowan for its leaves, deeply cut as in the Ash – it is sometimes called Mountain Ash – or for its fruits, bright red but invested with white magic,

> Rowan tree and red thread
> Haud the witches a' in dread;

or for its meditative habit, for it is a solitary tree, fond of standing by a mountain beck or burn. We may admire the Juniper, that stripling conifer, for its fragrance and choice of pleasant places to grow in, places as different as a chalk down and a Cumberland fell. Evelyn admired the Silver Birch for a juice tapped from its trunk and made into mead, according to a receipt sent by a fair lady. But we cannot agree that otherwise it is a despicable tree. It is a lover of light and space – I doubt if many Birches, or Birks, as they are called in the North, now grow at Birkenhead – but what we mainly commend is its silver bark. It is effectively cut by dark transverse lines, breathing-spaces, such as almost all trees have in some form, though they are not so conspicuous, except perhaps in the Alder and Elder. A pleasant way of studying them is to pull a cork, a piece of bark from the Cork Oak; we can see how the lines run round the cork, for if they ran up and down it would not be air-tight. In May the silver trunk is half-hidden

by the fresh foliage, helping the illusion that it is a white column
of water that rises to break in a falling fountain of green spray.
The best that Turner in his *Herbal* says of the tree is,

> I have not red of any vertue it hath in physick; howbeit, it serveth for
> many good uses, and for none better than for betynge of stubborn boys,
> that either lye or will not learn.

Yet it is so beautiful a tree that it almost seems a visitor to this
world. Perhaps it tries to get away from it, for, though Coleridge
calls it the Lady of the Woods, it has gone nearer to discovering
the North Pole than any other tree. It may have travelled even
farther, for, after they were drowned,

> The carline wife's three sons cam hame,
> And their hats were o' the birk.

Kilmeny too, when she returned from the land

> where the cock never crew,
> Where the rain never fell, and the wind never blew,

had on her head

> The bonny snood of the birk sae green.[8]

Here it does not live long, a hundred years or so, but the bark
may remain when the wood has rotted away; and when we find,
as we often do in a damp place, the empty sheath of bark, we
might imagine of the tree itself, that having now vanished,

> It neither grew in syke nor ditch,
>   Nor yet in ony sheugh;
> But at the gate o' Paradise
>   That birk grew fair eneugh.[9]

The Holly might seem to have a stronger claim to Paradise, as
more observant of Christmas, and answering better to the
Psalmist's description of the godly man, 'that will bring forth his
fruit in due season; his leaf also shall not wither'. But to keep
Christmas is not always a sign of grace, and the leaves do wither.
Holly sheds its leaves, but only so many each season, for, thinking
it a waste to use them for but one year, it retains them for three

8. Hogg: 'Kilmeny'.
9. 'The Wife of Usher's Well'.

or four. This of course is the practice with all evergreen trees; they are evergreen like our own genealogical trees, of which it is written, 'As the green leaves on a thick tree, some fall, and some grow; so is the generation of flesh and blood, one cometh to an end, and another is born'. In any case there is no great merit in being evergreen; one might be an evergreen liar like Maister Andro Kennedy's cousin, compared in a way to Holly:

> Willelmo Gray, sine gratia,
>   Myne awne deir cusing, as I wene,
> Qui nunquam fabricat mendacia,
>   Bot when the holyne growis grene.[10]

It may seem fantastic to suggest that a tree could tell a lie, but that is what some venerable churchyard Yews might be said to do; at least they present a spurious appearance of great antiquity. When a Yew is a few hundred years old, side shoots coalesce with the trunk, giving it an enormous girth; and often the inner wood dies away, leaving only

> A large throat, calling to the clouds for drink;[11]

but the tree is probably lying in its throat if it claims to be older than

> Those long-liv'd Oaks that call old *Nestor*, Boy;[12]

such Oaks as we see in Sherwood Forest, into whose hollow trunk holiday-makers disappear, changing to hamadryads. But there can be no falsehood about Irish Yews, for they are all derived from two trees discovered as seedlings in County Fermanagh about the middle of the Eighteenth Century; in fact, having all been propagated by cuttings, they might be said to be parts of those trees, like the scattered limbs of Osiris, for which Isis made a careful search. That they cannot reproduce themselves by seeds implies that they are varieties of the ordinary Yew. Several kinds of trees have produced varieties, and among them are two strangely different tendencies; some have branches that, starting to grow straight outwards, droop with their own weight, as in the Weeping Willow, which provided a pleasant shelter for

10. Dunbar.
11. Cowper: 'Yardley Oak'.
12. Cowley: *Liber Plantarum*.

Pope; others have branches that shoot upwards, as in the Lombardy Poplar,

> That like a feather waves from head to foot.[13]

The Irish Yew is of the second kind. Yews may have been planted in churchyards, places where their foliage would not poison horses, to provide wood for bows –

yew, of all things, is that whereof perfect shooting would have a bow made,

says Ascham – or to provide branches for a procession on Palm Sunday, as they did at Castle Dangerous; or they may have been a kind of Gospel Oak, themselves the preacher and the sermon; but if they were originally intended to be a substitute for the Cypress of the Romans,

> The only constant mourner o'er the dead,[14]

the modern tree answers to the purpose better than the old Yew. And more truthful about its age, it may be considered equally a 'reverend vegetable'. It is of old Yews, their dark foliage tipt with a light green in May, as though they were striving to renew their youth, that Lady Winchilsea makes the disparaging comparison:

> yews court the breeze,
> That, like some beaux whom time doth freeze,
> At once look old and young.[15]

Nowadays, when it is mostly elderly people who come to church, the youthful Irish Yews are to be commended for their frequent appearance in our churchyards.

How favourably the Irish Yew compares with the Euonymus or Spindle-tree! We might hesitate to look for its flowers in May, not only because we should be too soon, but also because Pliny says that too many presage a plague. Euonymus means Of a Good Name, but it is given to propitiate the tree; so the Furies at Colonus were called the Eumenides or Well-intentioned, and the Devil in Scotland was called the Gude Auld Man. No doubt

13. Leigh Hunt: 'The Story of Rimini'.
14. Byron: 'The Giaour'.
15. 'The Lord and the Bramble'.

the fear arose from its poisonous fruit, though no fruit looks prettier, like a priest's rose-red biretta at first, then splitting to expose the orange-coloured seeds. Turner, however, in naming the plant, thought only of the use to which its wood was put:

> it maye be called in englishe Spindle tree.

The Elder, whose flowers are also late, had an even worse reputation:

> Judas was hanged on an elder,

says Biron in *Love's Labour's Lost*, though Sir Thomas Browne, knowing his Bible better than that gay Frenchman, says,

That *Judas* perished by hanging himself, there is no certainty in Scripture.[16]

But if the Elder had a bad reputation, it is also true that no tree in the world had a better. *Anatomia Sambuci or The Anatomie of the Elder, Confirmed and Cleared by Reason, Experience and History – Gathered in Latine by Dr Martin Blochwich*, is the title of a book translated into English in the Seventeenth Century. In the Epistle Dedicatory the translator says of the author,

Here as in a curious Lantskip, he hath clearly and methodically represented to your view the Experiments and vertues of this humble Shrub; whether by chance discovered to the Commons, or by improvement to the rational. In whose ragged Cote are contained, I dare averr, rarer and safer Medicines, than the rob'd Indies enrich us with; and though they seem but homely; and the Products of Peasants, yet are more safe and effectual for our bodies and diseases, than the most renoued Exotericks.

Coles in his *Adam in Eden* also recommends the book, where, he says,

you may satisfie yourselfe perfectly of every particular. There is hardly a Disease from the Head to the Foot but it cures. It is profitable for the Head-ach, for Ravings and Wakings, Hypocondriack and Mellancholly, the Falling-sicknesse, Catarrhes, Deafenesse, Faintnesse and Feavours.

We can understand why the Host in *The Merry Wives of Windsor* called Doctor Caius his Aesculapius, his Galen, his heart of elder.

16. *Religio Medici.*

Even a fungus, often found on the tree, had its use. It is called Jew's-ear, but, as Sir Thomas Browne explains, it

concerneth not the Nation of the *Jews*, but *Judas Iscariot*, upon a conceit, he hanged on this Tree; and is become a famous Medicine in Quinsies, sore Throats, and strangulations ever since.[17]

The Elder looks a humble plant; we notice how gladly it springs up in any unoccupied place, perhaps a rabbit-bury, and how contentedly it grows in dismal surroundings; but it is said that the Dutch botanist, Boerhaave, never passed this wonderful plant without taking off his hat.

Other members of the Elder's family, if not so famous, are more attractive. Wayfaring-tree, named from the dusty appearance it still keeps even in days of dustless roads, may not bloom till June, but its flower-buds were visible all winter, protected only by hairs. Guelder-rose sets out to be attractive, for its flat cymes have a fringe of larger flowers, sterile and meant for show, though to our eyes giving the cymes a half-opened look. The Honeysuckles are even more unlike the Elder, though an inquisitive eye can detect a family resemblance in the flowers. Two rare Honeysuckles bloom in May, the naturalized Perfoliate, a climbing plant, and the Upright Fly, which stands, so to speak, on its own legs. These plants and myself were at one time more or less neighbours, but they affected me very differently. When I thought of the Perfoliate, or for that matter of the Common Honeysuckle, I felt depressed, but when I thought of the Upright Fly I was greatly cheered; in fact, it gave me a sense of my own uprightness. It was all due to a lady who drove her car down my street one day and, leaning out of the window, cried, 'Where does Mr Young live?' Where she lived, I knew; how indeed could I forget that imposing mansion on whose door-step I had stood, wondering whether to ring the bell or retreat in haste down the drive. But

> I laughed a wooden laugh
> That I could fear a door,[18]

and I rang the bell. When I came away a quarter of an hour later,

17. *Pseudodoxia*.
18. Emily Dickinson.

I hoped to see Field Sea-holly on Worthy Down – the object of my visit – but her I did not expect to see again. So that day, when I heard the voice crying like the voice of Wisdom in the street, 'Where does Mr Young live?' and, fearful what it might portend, rushed to the window, I was surprised to see who it was. Changing my carpet-slippers for shoes, I hastened downstairs, but there another surprise awaited me; the lady and the car had vanished, and a small elderly man stood at the door. He explained that she had gone to call on friends, and, as she would be back within an hour, had suggested that he might wait in my house. Inviting him to enter, I inquired his name, and 'Druce' he replied. Had it been the Apostle Paul I could not have been more astonished, nor, though I should not say so, more delighted. The name Druce added several cubits to his stature. An Edinburgh botanist once said to me, 'Druce is a subtle old boy; he describes exactly where a plant grows in a mountain corrie; you go there expecting to find it, but you don't; the description of the spot is accurate, only it applies to a different mountain'. He meant that willing to impart his knowledge, he was careful not to give away a rare plant. I felt half-afraid of him, this man who was born on the same day of the year as Linnaeus, but there was no need; in fact he was kind enough to tell me where I could find Burning Lobelia in the New Forest. 'Have you seen all the British plants?' I asked, and he replied that he had, though the last ten had given him a hard struggle. 'Are you the only botanist who has seen them all?' I went on, but he merely smiled. When I inquired about an Orchid so very rare that it has been seen only a few times, he modestly said that two of the times he had seen it himself. An hour slipped pleasantly past, but without the hoot of a car outside. Finding it necessary to seek a new topic of conversation, I spoke of an article he had written on the names of plants in Clare's poems. Somehow I had imagined Clare as living towards the end of the Eighteenth Century, so I was greatly astonished when he said that he had often seen Clare. 'When? Where?' I exclaimed, and he replied that as a boy he had seen him hanging about Northampton market-square. This started an interesting talk, and half an hour went by without my thinking of the car. When another subject became necessary, I said, 'I suppose you confine your attention to British plants?' But that was an unlucky shot, for 'Not altogether,' he replied, 'I hope to go to Brazil in the winter'. Still there was no sound of the car. In talking to this great man, I felt like one who starts to read *Paradise Lost* with enthusiasm, but after an hour or so finds it something of a strain. Yet I worried more about his wasting his time, for I had been told he wore elastic-sided boots, easily drawn on, to save a few seconds in the morning. At last we heard the car's hoot and went downstairs. 'By the way', he said at the door, 'do you happen to know where Upright Fly Honeysuckle grows near Amberley?' I did happen to know, and I told him. 'That's what I thought', he said; 'we shall look for it on the way back'. When I think how dependent I have been on botanists for my knowledge of plants, clinging to them as Perfoliate or Common Honeysuckle clings to a tree, I feel depressed; but when I think how I once directed Dr Druce, I feel like that small shrub, Upright Fly Honeysuckle.

9 The Fear of Flowers

People have been beheaded for various crimes, but no one, so far as I know, for picking a wild flower; yet such was almost my fate. One May evening, rowing from Henley to Wargrave, I left the main stream to find my way by a backwater. I spied a white flower on the bank, a flower I had not seen before, Summer Snowflake, commonly called Loddon Lily, though not a Lily but an Amaryllis. I picked it and laid it on the seat by the stern. Twilight was falling, deepened by the shade of trees, and the flower looked strangely white lying on the seat where, if I had had a companion, she would no doubt have sat. I began to think it was such a companion, and 'Amaryllis' I said softly. But Amaryllis made no reply. 'Amaryllis, you are a beautiful creature', I persisted; but Amaryllis remained silent. Though I had now to start rowing harder, for it was almost dark, I was about to renew my addresses, when I chanced to look round. I was just in time to fling myself forward; had I been a second or so later – for the boat was moving fast – I should no doubt have been beheaded by the low arch of a stone bridge. That the flower kept silent, nursing a grudge and anticipating revenge,

> Would seem incongruous as a singing tree,[1]

but it seemed so, as I lay that night in bed, between waking and sleep.

Cases of the kind, of a flower, as it were, hitting back, must be rare. Lord Bute, George III's Prime Minister, is said to have fallen when climbing a cliff for a plant near Christchurch, receiving injuries from which he afterwards died. But surely he was the last person against whom a wild flower would bear a grudge, for had he not produced a stupendous work, *Botanical tables*, *containing*

1. Crabbe: 'Resentment'.

the different Familys of British Plants, at a cost of £12,000? So we may consider it was only an accident. No doubt it was also an accident when the knight, plunging into a lake to procure a blue flower for his lady, was drowned, his last words being 'Forget me not'.[2] The improbability of the story – the Forget-me-not would be growing in about half an inch of water – mars its excellent moral, not to pick wild flowers. We can scarcely think of our native plants as capable of revenge. We have no such potent herbs as Medea gathered in Colchis, with which

she stayed the course of rushing rivers, and checked the stars and the paths of the sacred moon.[3]

Sometimes we see weeds almost choking corn, but would they

Pæonia mas.
Male Peionie.

2. Mills: *History of Chivalry*.
3. Apollonius Rhodius.

prevail, as Medea's herbs did, against that strange crop, the armed warriors who sprang up when Jason sowed the dragon's teeth?

Yet I am not so sure of the Peony. Though it is named after Paion, god of healing, sometimes identified with Apollo, so that a song in his praise is called a paean, the Peony is considered a dangerous plant to uproot. In this respect it resembles the strange Baaras, growing in the Jordan valley, of which Josephus says:

> They tie a dog to it and when the dog tries to follow him that tied it, the root is easily plucked up, but the dog dies immediately, as it were instead of the man that would take the plant away.[4]

Had he added that the plant shrieked, we might have thought it was that 'semi-homo', the Mandrake. The Peony has to be uprooted in the same way, some writers suggesting the dog should be tempted with a piece of meat. It grows wild on Steep Holme, an island in the Bristol Channel; it may however have been taken there, or shipwrecked like St Paul on Malta. Botanists visit it each May, and, though it is carefully guarded, contrive to carry away a bloom. It is said that a woodpecker, seeing anyone pick a Peony, strikes him blind; unfortunately there are no woodpeckers on that rocky island. That it resents a rabble of visitors as much as the screaming sea-gulls do, I am inclined to believe; certainly I had an unpleasant experience when I ventured to visit it for the second time. Being the only one who had made the journey before, I assumed leadership of the party, and on the way back collected the fares. 'Are you sure five shillings is enough?' they all asked, and as one who knew the ropes I smilingly assured them it was. But when we came ashore at Weston-super-Mare and I offered the collected sum to the boatmen, they looked at it with scorn; the fare had been raised by half-a-crown. Unable to make up the amount, I had to run after the others who were now dispersed, entering their cars or walking along the street. I could not help thinking that the Peonies on Steep Holme were tossing their rosy heads in laughter at my humiliation.

But when Clare speaks of the Fear of Flowers, he is not suggesting we should be alarmed; his sympathy is with the

4. *Wars of the Jews.*

plants, as the ones more likely to suffer. If I was nearly beheaded that evening when I was foolish enough

> To sport with Amaryllis in the shade,

I have known of a flower that was beheaded. Staying with friends in Streatham, I was invited one Sunday afternoon to go for a drive to Newlands Corner. 'Could you make it a wood near Dorking?' I asked. 'He's after some wild flower', said the husband. 'Let's help him to find it', said the wife. As we drove away I expatiated on the great rarity of the plant, Martagon Lily, hoping it might compensate for the popular charms of Newlands Corner. When we arrived at the place, the husband said he would stay by the car and smoke his pipe, but his wife said she would help me to look. It was a dark wood, darker after the blazing sunlight outside, and the first thing we did was to stumble over two lovers on the ground. When the same thing happened a few minutes later, she decided to rejoin her husband. I stuck, however, to my task, though I felt that the problems confronting the botanist in his laboratory were nothing to the problem of searching a Surrey wood on a Sunday afternoon. At last I gave it up and was returning to the road, when there, at the wood's edge, I saw what I was seeking, a Martagon Lily. It lay on the ground, the head half-severed from the stem. I looked about and discovered other plants, but all had completely lost their heads. I could understand someone picking a flower, but what maniac made a point of beheading Martagon Lilies? I rejoined my friends and showed them the plant with the half-severed head. The husband stared at it, but, far from being impressed, he laughed and said, 'You could have seen that in Streatham; it grows in our neighbour's garden'. I replied that no doubt it did, as it was not an uncommon garden flower. 'Then why did you come here to look for it?' he asked. As I could not think of an answer at the moment, in fact I am not sure I can think of one now, I smiled indulgently. 'I don't believe it is wild', he said. 'Some botanist must think so', I replied; 'he takes such great care of it that he cuts off its heads'. He pondered over the words, and then said, 'I give it up'. So I told him what I now remembered reading in a book, that a clergyman in the north of England, to save a rare Orchid from being picked or uprooted, made a practice each year of cutting off the heads.

Flowers might feel they have reason to fear. The plough has driven many to seek a refuge in hedges, and while they may gain additional protection in its thorns and prickles, they must view with some jealousy a field of Clover, engrossing so much of the bees' pleasant attention. Even flowers that were common in cornfields once are becoming scarce through cleaner cultivation. We seldom see Thorough-wax or Corn-cockle; yet Thorough-wax was so abundant in Gerard's day that he calls it an 'infirmitie', and Corn-cockle, the most beautiful of the Campions, has a name that means a weed. Damp-loving plants have suffered most, left high and dry by draining of the land; more than one flower is as extinct as Large Copper Butterfly. Cattle and those 'living lawn-mowers', sheep, tread down the flowers they do not eat; rare Orchids must have suffered heavy casualties. We have extended towns and tamed the surrounding country; I doubt if I should now find Sea-heath on the beach at Bexhill or Hoary Stock on the cliffs at Brighton. And of course flowers are picked; I cannot think what protects Grape Hyacinth growing on a bank outside Cambridge, or the beautiful Meadow Sage on a road-border not far from Oxford. If a flower is unattractive to the casual passer-by, plain looks being, so to speak, its saving grace, it will not escape the collector. I became so concerned about the protection of our wild flowers that I bought a book on the subject, *Wild Flower Preservation*; at least I thought it was on the subject, but it turned out to be taken up with the picking and pressing of flowers!

That of course is one way of preserving wild flowers, but we need a different way. Outside Gloucester we may notice a small useless-looking field with nothing in it better than Buttercups; but they are Serpent-tongued Spearworts, and those who bought the field to preserve the plant must have thought them worth their weight in gold. A doctor is usually considered justified in telling a lie to save a patient's life; would it be right to tell one to save a plant? I felt I knew the answer when I went one evening to Shoreham to look for Starry Clover. As I strolled along the beach, an angry man rushed up and asked if I knew I was trespassing. He spoke so sternly that I was about to apologize and turn away, when it occurred to me that I was doing nothing of the kind. A heated argument followed, but I had trespassed too often to be caught, so to speak, not trespassing at all. When he saw I meant to stand my ground – it was, in fact, what I was doing – he laughed and said, 'You are looking for Starry Clover; I had better show it to you, as you would find it in any case'. Leading me to a spot a little distance off, he explained that when the plant was in flower, he came down to the beach of an evening, and if he saw anyone wandering dangerously near, he told him he was trespassing. 'You are the first person who has not believed me', he added. When we parted as friends, I wished him luck in his good work of telling lies.

If a rare flower has anyone worse than a collector to fear, it is a person like myself, liable to fits of irrational behaviour. Staying one May in Somerset, I conceived an ambition to see Bristol Rock-cress. I knew someone who could help me, the Bristol botanist who the previous spring had entertained me to lunch and shown me a Rush; but could I ask him? In the intervening summer my relation to him became somewhat peculiar. There are one or two American plants found in Ireland and, except perhaps in Skye, nowhere else in Europe. Plato would have said they travelled across the lost Atlantis, but they may have come as seeds, sailing on a log or carried in the claws of a bird. One of them, Blue-eyed Grass, suddenly appeared on the Somerset coast, from which a few years later it disappeared. Its presence was a great secret, and when a botanist showed me this treasure, he said, 'For heaven's sake say nothing about it to —', and he named the Bristol botanist. These two were deadly enemies, each accusing the other of uprooting rare plants. The Bristol botanist, however, had somehow got wind of this plant, and most afternoons he arrived by train at the small town where I was staying. I feared to meet him, knowing that I should be closely questioned; so when I saw him coming along the street, I darted into a shop or, hastily retracing my steps, turned round a corner. I felt then it was not the way to treat a man at whose hospitable table I had sat, and how, when I wanted to see Bristol Rock-cress, could I have the conscience to ask his help? But wild flowers by this time had so demoralized me that I wrote him a letter. He replied, saying that as he was away from home, he would not have the pleasure of seeing me, but he enclosed directions for the plant, and added, 'It's on its last legs, but I can trust you not to touch it'. How little did he think I should tear it up by the roots.

When, following his directions, I arrived at the place, the Avon bank at Bristol, I saw a man stretched on the rock apparently asleep. Not wishing to disturb him, I circled round looking for the plant. It was a lonely spot in the sense that it was secluded by trees, and after I had softly approached him several times and withdrawn, I became aware that, though his eyes seemed shut, he was watching my movements with suspicion. He might have sat up and asked what I was doing, or of course I might have spoken and explained, but there seemed to be some point that neither of us was prepared to yield. Then, standing a little way above his head, I spied what I took to be the plant growing close beside him. Stepping down quickly I picked a flower, and, as I did so, his body quivered. He sprang to his feet with 'Here, you, what's your game?' but already I was scrambling down the slope. Safe on the road I saw it was Bristol Rock-cress, and I also saw with remorse I had torn up the little plant by the roots.

Greatly upset by what I had done, I craved for some kind of comfort; so I bought a tub of ice-cream and sat on a seat. When I had finished it I said to the Bristol Rock-cress, 'You may as well come home with me', and dropped it into the empty tub. But ice-cream does not soothe the troubled conscience, and I felt a desire to do some good deed. 'I will call on Agatha Miller', I said; 'yes, and I will take her one or two flowers that will give her pleasure', for I knew she was ill, very ill indeed. So I picked three Spring Cinquefoils; she would not mind my picking them, for, though rare, they are common on the Avon bank. These I also placed in the tub, and feeling more cheerful went my way.

She was lying by an open window that looked on the garden. Many wild flowers grew in that garden, a Romulea from Dawlish Warren, a Bird's-eye Primrose from Teesdale, a True Oxlip, perhaps from that beautiful Essex wood called Ugly. She did not share my scruples about collecting wild plants, if they were not too rare. 'You are a faddist', she once remarked. 'See, I have brought you a present', I said, holding up the ice-cream tub. She looked at it in surprise, but when I drew out the Cinquefoils, she smiled and said, 'How very kind'. Then she suddenly stared and said 'Oh', and I realized what I had done; in pulling out the Cinquefoils I had pulled out, entangled with them, the other plant. 'You have picked the Bristol Rock-cress', she cried; 'and you have torn it up by the roots'. I stood speechless; how could I explain about the man on the rock without appearing an utter fool? 'Perhaps I could plant it in your garden', I suggested. 'Yes, of course', she replied hopefully. I ran into the garden and dug a hole in the rockery with my fingers. 'Give it water', she called through the window. I went back into the house to ask for water, but seeing my hat in the hall I snatched it up instead and returned to the garden. From a tap at the side of the house I filled it with water, which I took and poured into the hole. She knew I did it for effect, for when, having filled up the hole, I turned, she was smiling sarcastically. 'I hope it will live', I said. 'I hope it will', she replied. But whether it lived or not, she herself did not live to know.

10 Botanists and Botanophils

Though a person caught trespassing cannot be prosecuted (in spite of lying notices) perhaps he ought to be; so seldom is there any reason for being caught. When we trespass in a wood, we should walk quietly as in a church – Dryden speaks of 'a religious wood' – and aim at hearing rather than being heard; otherwise we may cause annoyance to the rightful owner – chittering squirrel or screaming jay. The art of trespassing on mountains asks a different kind of caution; it is more akin, I suppose, to the art of deer-stalking. Yet it is one thing to preach and another to practise, and I confess I have sometimes been arrested by an angry voice, 'Do you know you are trespassing?' Though the question usually admits of the simple answer 'Yes', I prefer to side-track it and explain that I am a botanist. While this produces no effect on a gamekeeper, a man I greatly admire for his devotion to duty, it may soothe a landlord who would not be thought unsympathetic towards any scientific pursuit. I have even known it lead to an invitation to tea. Unfortunately the explanation is not true.

Augusta Dallas and I are a pair; in fact if I had lived in the Eighteenth Century I should probably have married her; but as it was she fell into the hands of her Preceptor Husband. Crabbe tells in his Tale how this husband tried to teach her botany:

> He show'd the various foliage plants produce,
> Lunate and lyrate, runcinate, retuse;
> Long were the learned words, and urged with force,
> Panduriform, pinnatifid, premorse,
> Latent, and patent, papulous, and plane –
> 'Oh!' said the pupil, 'it will turn my brain'.

Augusta and I have cared for none of these things,

> And loves of plants, with all that simple stuff
> About their sex, of which I know enough.

Very likely he tried also to teach her the botanical names of plants; but 'Don't worry about them, dear', I should have said; 'I don't know them myself'. I have found it a disadvantage in talking to botanists not to know their language, but I am no worse than the ordinary Englishman who travels on the Continent. One woman told me it was a shame that with my classical education I had not learnt what she called the proper names of plants. Having heard her say these names, 'Perhaps I should mispronounce them', I replied, but I doubt if she saw the point of the remark. Only Coles has made me regret my ignorance, for, as he says,

what a pleasant thing it is for a Man (whom the Ignorant thinks to be alone) to have plants speaking Greek and Latine to him.

That I am not a botanist is so true that even to say so would have an air of untruth; but might I not find a place among the botanophils? Linnaeus drew a distinction between a botanist, one who describes and classifies plants, and a botanophil, one who studies their anatomy or physiology; but as the distinction no longer holds, for both would now be called botanist, the term botanophil may be borrowed to describe a person who, without being a botanist, is interested in plants. But perhaps this new distinction should first be made clear.

While a botanophil searches for plants, a botanist may not have time to do so, or even the interest. One day on the Gogmagog Hills I asked a man to direct me to Wandlebury Camp. 'Come along', he said, 'I am going that way myself'. Being of an inquisitive nature, I soon discovered he was a Cambridge botanist. Now some distance along the road was growing a rare plant, Perennial Flax, that would have caught the eye of any botanophil. I had found it a few minutes before and was still excited. When we came to the spot I expected him to make a remark; but no, he would have passed it by. On my pointing it out, he peered at it through his spectacles, not without some interest, and said, 'Well, really, though I often come this way, I never noticed it before'. I suppose he was too much taken up with botany. Sachs in his

History of Botany speaks of 'that dull occupation of plant-collectors', and appears to regard it as outside, if not beneath, the botanist's interest. Usually a botanist's place is by the microscope, his field of vision a slide, his flowers iodine stains. It is pleasantly said that some botanists would not know a Daisy if they met it in a field; only when they had taken it to their laboratory, pressed and dried it, and spread it on paper, would they exclaim 'Ah, Bellis perennis'. We like to think that the specialist overreaches himself and is in some way stupider than ourselves. We should remember that idiot means literally one who is not a specialist, but an amateur or layman. Our uninstructed eyes may admire what they see, on a bank of Violets, or in a garden:

> But he, the man of science and of taste,
> Sees wealth far richer in the worthless waste,
> Where bits of lichen and a sprig of moss
> Will all the raptures of his mind engross.[1]

The botanophil is so much a plant-seeker that in winter, when there are few plants to find, he usually hibernates. Indeed it is by this habit of hibernating that he may be best distinguished. While the botanist is like an evergreen, working throughout the year, the botanophil is like one of those perennials that die down to a rootstock in autumn and lie more or less dormant till the spring. A botanophil once confessed to me that in winter he could not remember the botanical names. But in spring, before the Wake-robin is itself awake, he is up and doing, wandering about in his eager search for plants; Demeter did not search more earnestly for Persephone. He is glad to greet old friends, such as Primrose and Violet, but his great desire is to make new acquaintances. Some plants, however, are shy and retiring, keeping themselves to themselves, as we say, and he may need an introduction. Probably he finds someone to give him the introduction, for one botanophil helps another. The whereabouts of a rare plant may be a sworn secret, but some people think a secret is kept if they entrust it to someone else to keep; and so the information spreads. An old woman who lived on a Yorkshire moor told me that one day a car drew up at her cottage and the occupants asked to be directed to a certain spot on the moor. A few days later another

1. Clare: 'Shadows of Taste'.

car arrived and there was the same request. Car followed car for a month or more. Next summer the same thing happened, but after that the cars ceased to come. 'What did they want?' she asked plaintively. I explained that no doubt a rare plant had been discovered on the moor, but it had been so much picked that it had disappeared. I think she scarcely understood, for she shook her head with 'It's very queer'. The picking of plants is the besetting sin of botanophils. They forget the part of the Catechism that says, 'What is thy duty towards thy neighbour? . . . . To keep my hands from picking and stealing'. Too often they are less like Demeter than Hades who ravished her daughter from the earth. Blue Toadflax at one time grew in the crevices of Winchester's walls, but if anyone now asks, 'Ubi est ille Toad-in-the-hole?' the answer is 'Non est inventus'.

Of course there is no clear dividing line between botanist and botanophil; the one species runs into the other as Sloe into Bullace. How should we classify John Gough of Kendal, of whom Wordsworth writes:

> No floweret blooms
> Throughout the lofty range of these rough hills,
> Nor in the woods, that could from him conceal
> Its birth-place; none whose figure did not live
> Upon his touch?[2]

Unless we make an allowance for his being blind, perhaps we should put him among the botanophils. Yet we are told that feeling the stem with his fingers, the flower with his tongue and the hairs with his lower lip, he could identify any strange plant. When Moss Campion, that spreads its painted mat on mountain-tops, was put in his hand, he said at once, 'I have never examined this plant before, but it is Silene acaulis'. As a rule, however, the resemblance between botanist and botanophil is superficial, though most people confuse the two species. In fact usually, when I speak of a botanist, what I mean is a botanophil.

But superficial as the resemblance may be, I fear it is enough to deprive me of a place among the botanophils. My ignorance of botanical names is itself a kind of outer darkness. Walking one day on a South Devon beach I met a man who was peering

2. 'The Excursion'.

earnestly at the shingle. Passers-by, supposing he had lost
something, stopped to have a look too, but from a tin box, slung
on his back, called a vasculum, the Black Maria of many a rare
and beautiful plant, I judged he was a botanophil. When I asked
if he was looking for any particular plant, he replied he was
looking for – but the Latin name was Greek to me. I am like Sir
Thomas Browne:

> I know most of the Plants of my Countrey, yet methinks I do not
> know as many as when I did but know a hundred, and had scarcely ever
> Simpled further than Cheap-side.[3]

At that time I thought I knew most plants, enough at least to
recognize a rare plant if I saw it. So I offered to help him, an offer
he did not accept at all graciously. As we walked along the beach,
we began to talk about plants, but we only began, for if on that
subject I had little Latin, he had less English. He was like
Erasmus, so learned that he had forgotten his own language, or
like Chatterton's Knyghte, Syr John:

> Whoever speketh Englysch ys despysed,
> The Englysch hym to please moste fyrst be latynized.

One might have thought that his ignorance of English names and
mine of Latin would have made us quits, but far from it; he
regarded my ignorance as a personal affront. He asked sarcastic
questions, such as, Why did I look for plants when I did not
know their names? and Did I know what I was supposed to be
looking for now? It was clear that he wanted to get rid of me, but
I stuck to him like a bur. As he still failed to find the plant, he
grew more and more irritable, but I refused to be shaken off. I
saw he was putting up with my hateful presence only till we
should reach the end of the beach, but that was all I asked. When
we arrived there I said, 'Will you tell me the name of a plant on
the other side of the road? I think it is only a garden escape'.
Grudgingly he followed me up from the beach, but when his
eyes lighted on the plant, he burst into laughter. 'You, you,' he
spluttered through his laughter, 'fancy you finding the Corrigiola!' So that was what we had been looking for, this pretty
little plant, perhaps, as I learnt afterwards, in its last haunt in

3. *Religio Medici.*

England; Corrigiola, Little Shoe-string, left behind by I wonder what sea-nymph.

Another thing that makes botanophils shut the door against me is my ignorance of botany. To a botanist their knowledge may seem of no great account, but for me

> Oh, the little more, and how much it is!
> And the little less, and what worlds away![4]

The contemptuous treatment I received on that South Devon beach was nothing to what I experienced from a Cornish botanophil. When I called on him as a stranger he welcomed me warmly, so warmly indeed that I felt I had to explain, 'I am not really a botanist; my interest in plants is only sentimental'. 'I quite understand', he said approvingly, and asked if there was any plant I wished to see. 'Yellow Star-thistle', I suggested. 'You mean Centaurea solstitialis', he said, and began to unfold a map. Then reflecting a moment he went on, 'Perhaps I had better take you to the place'. 'Please do not trouble', I said. 'No trouble at all', he replied; 'I want to go there myself'. When he explained that it meant a considerable journey by train, I felt embarrassed by his kindness. Next day on the journey he proved himself to be a most agreeable companion; when I spoke of some rare plants I had found, mentioning among others Corrigiola, 'I see you know a good deal', he said. When we arrived at our destination, he told me the plant was small and we should have to search carefully. We drifted some distance apart in our search, and, chancing to look his way, I noticed he was kneeling on the ground. 'He has found it', I thought; but no, he rose and continued to search. A few minutes later I saw him kneeling again, and this time he appeared to be digging a hole; what more he was doing I could not see, for his back was towards me. Several times the same thing happened; there was nothing furtive about the action, but I was never near enough to make out what he was about. At last he cried, 'Here it is', and running over I saw Yellow Star-thistle. 'I am glad we found it', he said, as we started to walk back to the station. So he said, but what I kept asking myself was, Why had he come all this way to dig little holes in the ground? A light broke on me in the train. As we passed the

4. Browning: 'By the Fireside'.

place where we had searched for the Star-thistle, looking out of the window he remarked, 'We find some rare aliens there'. 'Oh, really', I said, but what I thought was, 'And you are the one who finds them; and you find them for the simple reason that you plant them; so you gain a reputation for yourself. You would not have let anyone else see you planting them today; but of course I do not count'. And I thought of that haughty queen who did not mind undressing before her male attendants, regarding them as beneath her contempt.

Gerard writes in his *Herbal*,

The male Peionie groweth wilde upon a cony berry in Betsome, being in the parish of Southfleet in Kent, two miles from Graves-end;

whereupon his editor, Johnson, comments,

I have been told that our Author himselfe planted the Peionie there, and afterwards seemed to find it there by accident.

Most botanophils regard it as a serious crime to introduce plants, interfering with our native flora. But when I think how they themselves interfere with it, picking and uprooting plants, I should not mind committing the crime myself. Unfortunately I do not know how to set about it; I am not even a gardener.

11 June Orchids

W. H. Hudson tells of an atheist who went to an Orchid show and came away believing in the Devil. As I have not carried my theological studies as far as an Orchid show, I can speak only of our native Orchids, and of these I think the character can be cleared. I should make, however, one exception, Twayblade.

Even our common Orchids, Early Purple, Spotted and Greenwinged, people regard with a peculiar interest, as though they were not merely beautiful or curious, but also a little wicked. But if their flowers are queer, it is because they are specialized, designed to admit certain insects and exclude the rest. Sometimes dark stains on their leaves give them a sinister look, but we may see such stains on the Cuckoo-pint. Perhaps they serve to attract attention, like the black patches women once wore on their faces. Or perhaps they serve to frighten away grazing animals; the leaves themselves, full of sharp crystals, are already well protected against snails. If Tertullian could say

A single floweret from the hedgerow, I say not from the meadows, will, I presume, prove to you that the Creator was no sorry artificer,[1]

why should these Orchids, fearfully and wonderfully made, suggest the Devil?

There are, however, three less common kinds, whose purpose like the Devil's seems to be to deceive: Bee, Fly and Early Spider. There is no doubt about the counterfeit likeness to an insect; when I asked a child to touch a Bee Orchid he turned away. Langhorne tells how he was taken in:

> See, on that floweret's velvet breast
> How close the busy vagrant lies;

1. *Against Marcion.*

but when he came nearer –

> I sought the living Bee to find,
> And found the picture of a Bee.[2]

Does the counterfeit attract insects? One botanist says that flies can be seen patiently licking the effigy on a Fly Orchid, male flies no doubt, who mistake it for a female. Or does it repel them? Another botanist, cutting off a Bee Orchid's effigy, laid it on a Peony, with the result that bees approaching swerved away, like people who come to a theatre and find the notice House Full. The character of these plants is best cleared on the view that the likeness is accidental, and for an insect does not exist. If there is any deception, it has not paid. The Bee Orchid pollinates itself, a fact which Darwin, great admirer of cross-fertilization, is said to have so deplored that he expressed the wish that he might live a few thousand years to see the Bee Orchid become extinct – the end to which he thought the plant's habit would lead. Bee Orchids, however, are not yet uncommon; but the Fly Orchid is scarce, and the Early Spider one of the rarest plants. Certainly the likeness is not profitable for them so far as we are concerned, for who can resist picking a flower that looks like an insect? Walking one April day with a friend across a field near Brighton, I suddenly stopped. My friend stared at me in astonishment and said, 'Do you always stop and throw your hat in the air when you see a Dandelion?' I replied it was not a Dandelion I was looking at, but an Early Spider Orchid. I went on to explain that this particular field had long been famous for the plant. Children on their way to school had occasionally picked it, struck by its resemblance to a spider. This had come to the ears of a botanist, who, anxious to protect it, had gone to the school and lectured the children on the wickedness of picking so rare and precious a flower. The result was that the children, wishing not to miss anything, had made a systematic search for it, picking every flower they could find. It was thought they had exterminated the plant; the discovery that at least one Early Spider Orchid survived was the reason for my transport.

The Late Spider Orchid, which blooms in summer, might seem to practise a double deception, not only resembling an insect but trying to pass itself off as a Bee Orchid. Looking for

2. 'The Bee-flower'.

it in one of the few places where it is found, perhaps blown across the English Channel as a dusty seed, I should not have distinguished it from the Bee Orchids among which it grew without a botanist's help. But of course I do not examine flowers closely; I should feel it an impertinence, like saying to a woman, 'Madam, may I look at your face through a magnifying-glass?' In the case of the other Orchids with animal names, there can be no deception. The Butterfly Orchid would flatter itself if it imagined its flowers were more like Cabbage Butterflies than small white moths; but it is too well acquainted with moths to do so; it is for them its flowers glimmer in the dusk and shed their scent. The scent of a plant is said to be a by-product, but what enchanted nights the by-product of Small Butterfly Orchid and White Habenaria gave me one June in Mull! In the Frog Orchid I can detect no likeness to its namesake, but then I have

Serapias Batrachites.
Frog Satyrion.

never been able to see the Man in the Moon. The Lizard Orchid, tall and untidy, does not readily recall the nimble reptile that vanishes in the grass with a wriggle; but few people have the chance of making the comparison. Though it persists in one or two places, even on a Somerset golf-course, it approaches the extinction of that ancient winged lizard, the pterodactyl. The Monkey Orchid is also a poor ape. A beautiful blue flower, it suggests a monkey chiefly in the care with which it is guarded. Padlocked gate and barbed wire, however, are intended not to keep the Monkey in but to keep the trespasser out. There is also a notice-board where it grows, that threatens him with prosecution. Such a warning frightens me, for as a child I confused prosecution with persecution, and I cannot yet disentangle the two ideas in my mind. I may have been deterred too by the thought of what has happened to others: Linnaeus shot at by Laplanders, suspicious of a stranger, Sherard by a mountaineer who mistook him for a wolf, Tournefort almost beaten to death by villagers who thought he was robbing their orchards. But the Thames Valley that June morning appeared so peaceful that I felt reassured, and, grateful for the notice-board's warning, I took a good look-round before climbing the gate to find the flower. The only other Orchid in which a likeness may be detected is the Green Man. It shows us a gallows from which a number of green men are being hanged; perhaps they are the souls of people who in their lifetime picked Green Man Orchids.

There are one or two Orchids on which, considering their manner of life, a strict moralist might frown. The main function of plants, as we view them, is to manufacture food from air and water. Only green plants, we might almost say, can do it, and it is on the food they make that all animals, including ourselves and fish, directly or indirectly subsist.

All flesh is grass, is not onely metaphorically, but litterally, true; for all those creatures we behold, are but the herbs of the field, digested into flesh in them, or more remotely carnified in our selves.[3]

> Why grasse is greene, or why our blood is red,
> Are mysteries which none have reach'd unto;[4]

3. Sir Thomas Browne: *Religio Medici*.
4. Donne: 'Of the Progresse of the Soule'.

but we know at least that it is on the green that the red depends. So we are apt to look askance at plants that are not green, as though they were shirking their proper task. Bird's-nest Orchid, not uncommon in Beech-woods, is such a plant, for it is as brown as a naked Indian. It is not a parasite, for it does not prey on living plants, but feeds on decayed vegetation with the help of a fungus in its nest-like roots. Orchids, like Heather and other plants, depend on the help of friendly fungi; even great trees often do, as witness the Toadstools, their fruits, that come up in woods; yet it seems a shame that an Orchid should descend to such a manner of life. But after all it is our own manner of life,

> for who ever sawe
> A man of leaves, a reasonable tree?[5]

There is one respect in which Orchids as a family have a bad reputation; they are, as Culpeper says, 'under the dominion of Dame Venus'. Satyrs ate their tubers to excite a lawless love passion, so that an old name for Orchid is Satyrion:

> But our cold maids do dead men's fingers call them,[6]

suggesting rather that like the White Water-lily they would allay such a passion. And, as it happens, there are no satyrs in this country, though there are more than forty kinds of Orchid. We cannot think they possess this wicked virtue; the only feeling they are likely to arouse is an affection for themselves. We admire the prim Orchid called Pyramid, though we may criticize its ideas of solid geometry; we feel hurt that Fragrant Orchid, rose-coloured and scented, should be named by botanists Gymnadenia, Naked Glands; we regret that the very pretty Burnt Orchid, sometimes called the Dwarf, spreads its patches of brown fire on so few of our chalk hills; we wish that White Helleborine, or Egg Orchid, were not so shy and would open its flowers; but they are eggs that seldom open. Even satyrs might be overawed by the beauty of Lady Orchid (Orchis purpurea). But 'each man kills the thing he loves', it is said, and Lady Orchid has been so persecuted that it is a kind of Virgin Martyr. Anne Pratt speaks of it as common in her day, but now it lives the life of an

5. Giles Fletcher: 'Christ's Victorie in Heaven'.
6. *Hamlet.*

anchorite in one or two woods. It was with little hope of finding this chaste plant (my father called a thing chaste when he meant beautiful, as though the two ideas were much akin) that I arrived one day at a small town in Kent. Vaguely walking along a road, I stopped some countrymen to ask if they knew of a rare Orchid which I attempted to describe. They said they knew it quite well, but on further inquiry I saw they were thinking of some common Orchid. Then suddenly something made me open my eyes and say, 'What a piece of luck!' From a building along the road young men were pouring out; I knew who they were, students of an Agricultural College, and 'Who more likely to give me the information?' I thought. I stopped the first group, but they shook their heads. Anxious to help, however, they halted the next group and put the matter to them. Other groups joined us to learn what was going on, till the road was blocked by the assembly. But the whole Agricultural College failed me. I was watching the crowd move towards the town, when a student ran back to tell me that a few days before he had seen a man with a vasculum cross a field and enter a wood by a gate, which he pointed out. Clutching at a straw, I started to follow this Invisible Man across the field. The gate had a notice, sternly warning trespassers, and I wondered at the man's effrontery in ignoring it, as I too passed this barrier. If he was invisible when I crossed the field, I cannot describe what he was in that pathless wood. Yet in the end, after much wandering about and in a different wood, I tracked him down, or, if not the man, Lady Orchid.

So the character of all our Orchids might seem cleared, were it not for the extraordinary conduct of a Twayblade. A Lecturer in Botany, whose acquaintance I had made, took me in his car one day to see a certain plant, and as we drove back said, 'Have you ever seen—?' The moment he mentioned the name I cried, 'Surely it does not grow about here?' 'Oh yes, it does', he replied with a smile, 'I can take you to the place now'; and he stopped and turned his car. Once in Scotland a friend had introduced me to his sister with 'She knows all the wild flowers'; but when I asked her about Small Twayblade, an elusive little plant that hides under bracken, she confused it with Common Twayblade, which you might find in almost any wood. I laughed as I recalled that; this time I knew I should see the plant, for a Lecturer in Botany does not make such a mistake. At last the car stopped and we got out. 'Here it is', he said, and I found myself staring at a Common Twayblade. 'But it's a Common Twayblade', I said blankly. 'I don't know what you mean by a Common Twayblade, but this is Listera ovata', he replied. Listera ovata, Common Twayblade – that indeed was what he had said, but as it had not occurred to me that anyone could think so poorly of my knowledge of plants as to suppose I wanted to see Common Twayblade, I had mistaken Listera ovata for Listera cordata, Small Twayblade. Twayblade gets its name from two broad lip-like leaves, from which, a mere tip at first but lengthening out, its flower-stalk projects. Though such a phenomenon seems to have been unnoticed by botanists, I had a distinct impression that the Twayblade shot out its tongue.

12   A Good Guide

Wild flowers are our best guide to Great Britain. If they have
taught me no botany, they have taught me geography; mountains, hills, forests, rivers, I know them as well as a schoolboy;
better indeed, having seen them for myself. And like a good
guide they include everything. Once I met an American who
told me he had come to this country to see its famous golf-
courses; I found them a subject on which I could speak with
knowledge, for does not Matted Sea-lavender grow on the golf-
course at Hunstanton, Striated Catchfly at Littlehampton, while
at Sandwich –? But a guide should begin with London.

Gwendolen in Oscar Wilde's play says,

> I had no idea there were any flowers in the country.

It is usually supposed that the only flowers she was familiar with
were expensive ones from florists, but considering the title of the
play, *The Importance of Being Earnest*, I prefer to think she was a
botanist who for some reason confined her studies to London.
And why not? Did not Lord de Tabley find in the month of
August, 188 wild plants in Hyde Park? I wonder if Gwendolen
was as much puzzled as I was by a strange yellow flower growing
in some western streets. Probably not, for being a botanist she
would identify it as the South American Galinsoga and guess it
had escaped from Kew. But I doubt if she found the yellow flower
that shot up so profusely after the Great Fire, making a golden
fire of its own, London Rocket.

London is not the only town that has given its name to a wild
flower. Nottingham Catchfly still appears in the neighbourhood
of Nottingham Castle, where it was first identified, but probably
it would be vain to search Deptford for Deptford Pink. Bristol
Rock-cress can be found at Bristol, though with difficulty, but

Bath Asparagus is plentiful about Bath, where its young shoots are sold in the market. (Its other name, Spiked Star of Bethlehem, recalls that eastern town, where

> The wise men did by star-light seek the Sun.[1]

At Oxford no one can fail to see Oxford Ragwort; in spite of its botanical name, Senecio squalidus, which might be translated Squalid Old Man, its cheerful yellow flowers enliven the city walls through most of the year. But anyone who sets off by train from London to see it may as well stop at Ealing; he will already have seen it outside Paddington Station. Plants travel a good deal by rail, some as seeds making long journeys in trucks, others blown along the line by the gust of a passing train. The Squalid Old Man, travelling by rail, has visited not only London, but such distant places as Warwick and Winchester.

Flowers do of course grow in the country, though Gwendolen was surprised to see them; but so far as wild flowers are concerned, one might do well enough in towns. Take Aldeburgh, a small town, half a town, you might say, the other half having been swept away by the sea, as witness the Town Hall standing almost on the beach:

> Here the strong Mallow strikes her slimy root,
> Here the dull night-shade hangs her deadly fruit;
> On hills of dust the henbane's faded green,
> And pencil'd flower of sickly scent is seen;
> At the wall base the fiery nettle springs,
> With fruit globose and fierce with poison'd stings;
> Above (the growth of many a year) is spread
> The yellow level of the stone-crop's bed;
> In every chink delights the fern to grow,
> With glossy leaf and tawny bloom below:
> These, with our sea-weeds, rolling up and down,
> Form the contracted Flora of the town.[2]

But wild flowers are a guide not only to towns but to all places of interest. Tuberous Thistle takes us to Avebury, where we see ancient stones and an earthwork of which Aubrey says:

1. Quarles: *Emblems*.
2. Crabbe: 'The Borough'.

This old monument does as much exceed in greatness the so renowned Stoneheng, as a Cathedral doeth a parish Church.

If we go to the New Forest to look for Lungwort we shall probably find ourselves at Beaulieu Abbey. Lungwort, which gets its name from white blotches on the leaves suggesting a cure for consumption, was no doubt used by the monks, though it was not discovered by botanists till the Seventeenth Century. If we happen to be in the north of England, either of two rare plants, the deadly Baneberry, sometimes called Herb Christopher, or the insipid Mountain Currant, might lead us to Rievaulx Abbey. Perhaps places of literary interest appeal to us; in that case, if our search for wild plants does not take us to London, it will almost certainly take us to the Lake District. A sure and easy way to see Wild Tulip is to pay a visit to William Morris's garden at Kelmscott, where, once carefully cherished by the poet, it now survives him like his poems. If we should happen to be romantically minded, we are blessed indeed if Birthwort guides our steps to Godstow Priory. The nuns, those holy midwives, must have used the plant that still grows abundantly in their forsaken garden, but it is not of births we shall think, but of a burial. Somewhere under our feet lies the Fair Rosamond, according to the epitaph ('nothing answerable to her beauty', says Camden):

> Hac jacet in tumba rosa mundi non Rosamunda,
> Non redolet, sed olet, quae redolere solet –
>
> Rosa mundi – the world's rose – lies in this tomb,
>   Not Rosamunda – a pure rose;
> She smells not sweetly now, but stinks,
>   She who was wont to smell so sweetly.

Carlyle quotes his Teufelsdröckh,

Some time before Small-pox was extirpated, there came a new malady of the spiritual sort on Europe: I mean the epidemic, now endemical, of View-hunting, –

Carlyle adding the comment 'How true!' As this epidemic has not abated but rather increased, we expect plants to take us to vantage-points, from which we can best view the scenery; and in this they do not fail. Unless we feel like the decadent poet,

> I am so tired of holly-sprays
> And weary of the bright box-tree,[3]

we shall climb Box Hill,

> whither the ladies, gentlemen, and other water-drinkers from the neighbouring Ebesham Spaw, often resort during the heat of summer, and divert themselves in the natural alleys and shady recesses, among the Box-trees.[4]

Things have changed since Evelyn's time; no water-drinkers now go to Epsom or come from it, and the people who resort to Box Hill mostly sit on the open hillside, drinking with their eyes the distant Weald. But so many suffer from this epidemic of View-hunting, that, like a patient who prefers a private ward in a hospital, we may keep to the back of the hill. Perhaps we shall follow the favourite walk of George Meredith, one poet who preferred wild flowers – 'my wild ones!' – to the 'prim little scholars' of the garden. We shall see not only Holly-sprays, but in their natural state bright Box-trees. Having stept over clipt Box-hedges in gardens, we may be surprised at their size. Even so we may wonder how they made boxes, unless we remember that boxes were usually small objects, box and pyx being much the same word. We may not have known they had such nice flowers, but in spring at least

> All day in the sweet box-tree the bee for pleasure hummeth.[5]

Our view at the back of the hill will be restricted, but we shall see what to my northern eyes is perhaps the pleasantest sight in England, a chalk hill covered with dark Yews, and among them

> Flashing as in gusts the sudden-lighted whitebeam.[6]

Wild flowers are so much the best guide to the Highlands that they may be said to be the only guide. Of the thousands of people who set off each summer for John o' Groats few are destined to see the Highlands. They imagine them to be mountains, but as Geikie explains in *The Scenery of Scotland*, they are an enormous plateau, deeply cut by low glens and lochs. Anyone will realize

3. Dowson after Verlaine.
4. Sylva.
5. Bridges: 'April, 1885'.
6. Meredith: 'Love in the Valley'.

that who takes the hour's walk, mostly on the level, from Cairngorm to Ben Muich-dhui. People see as much of the Highlands by driving through the glens as we should see of a table by crawling on the floor. Plants draw us up to where, as though the rain and mist were not enough, they live by splashing burn and dripping rock-ledge. They guarantee no view, for not every day is clear, or has only

> White mist around the hollows of the hills,
> Phantoms of frith or lake.[7]

But mist has its compensations, being in fact a kind of field-glass, limiting the view no doubt, but making things look large and bright. As for the plants themselves, they are mostly charming dwarfs with evergreen leaves and cheerful flowers.

Caryophyllata alpina pentaphyllæa.
Fiue leafed Auens.

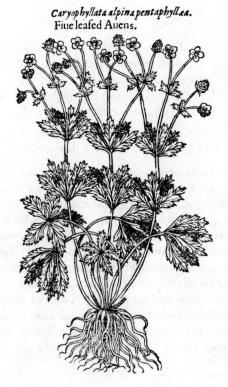

7. W. Allingham: 'Late Autumn'.

They are Arctic plants, and certainly they can endure great cold; Moss Campion can emerge alive from a melting block of ice. The remains of some of them have been found as far south as Devon, driven thither, we may suppose, in the Ice Age. After the ice retreated and other plants invaded the land, they withdrew to the North, where they survive with an Arctic animal, the blue mountain hare. But why take the trouble to go to the Highlands to see these plants, or even to the Lake District or Teesdale or Wales? Moss Campion, Purple Saxifrage, Bearberry, Mountain Avens, we can see them in our own or a neighbour's rockery. Of course we shall not miss the Highlands by not going there; if it be true,

> To make a prairie it takes a clover and one bee, –
> And revery.
> The revery alone will do
> If bees are few,[8]

We shall see the Highlands well enough without leaving our street. If we can make a mountain of a mole-hill, why not of a rockery? We might even reconstruct the Ice Age, clearing up points still obscure to the botanist. So much so that we have only to look at a rockery with these Arctic plants, and

> This landscape where the cuckoo shouts
> Will be the North Pole then or thereabouts.[9]

Except for birds perhaps, wild flowers are our only guide to quiet country places, those places where, if we are silent ourselves, some shy wild animal may be unsuspicious of our presence. How poor are all guide-books to Great Britain, unable to show us a blue mountain hare or even an otter! To see an otter is to see England. One day a botanist said, 'You will see Spring Snow-flake, but keep your eyes open; you are sure to see an otter'. So having found the plant I sat by a Quantock stream, enduring the cold March wind, to wait for the otter. I knew I should see it, for Spring Snowflake is much rarer as a plant than an otter is as an animal. I fixed my eyes on a bend of the stream, round which something told me it would come. I could see it already in

8. Emily Dickinson.
9. Anon.

imagination, swimming and being swept along with the current, like a person both walking and being carried down an escalator. I can see it still in memory, its fierce face rising among the ripples; I can see it now as clearly as the Snowflake; in fact it is hard to believe I did not really see an otter.

Wild flowers of course cannot afford to ignore altogether the more popular resorts, such as seaside towns, waterfalls, caverns and such like. So we find that to see White Rock-rose waving in the wind on Brean Down we have to pass through Weston-super-Mare. Alternatively we could pass through Torquay to see it at Babbacombe. To see Cotoneaster we make our way through Llandudno to the Great Orme. Spring Gentian takes us up Teesdale, and we should feel mean not to pay our pence to visit that famous waterfall, High Force. Cheddar Gorge, with its much-advertised caverns, is not to be avoided, for nowhere else can we see Cheddar Pink.

> O dinna think, my pretty pink,
> But I can live without thee,[10]

says Burns; but he was thinking merely of a woman, not of a wild flower. We borrow the name Pink not only to denote a colour, but also to express the acme of something; Mercutio calls himself 'the very pink of perfection'. So it is not surprising that the Cheddar Pink, too tempting not to be picked or uprooted, remains now on but a few inaccessible rocks. That is what I thought at least, till I offered to show it to a rheumatic old lady. When we drove up the Gorge and 'Stop' I cried to her chauffeur, she looked at the cliff and said, 'Don't tell me I have to climb up there'. But that was what I did tell her. Though I helped her as best I could, supporting and dragging her, she appeared to hold me responsible for the steepness of the slope. At last I brought her to a point where we could see a few Pinks growing on a rock. 'But can't I get to them?' she asked. 'Surely you don't want to pick them,' I protested. 'Certainly not,' she replied. 'You just want to examine them?' I suggested. 'No, I don't want to examine them,' she surprised me by answering testily. 'Then what do you want?' I asked. 'I want to touch one,' she replied. Extraordinary, I thought; what strange tenderness is this that makes her want to

10. Song: 'Here's to Thy Health'.

touch a wild flower? Then I remembered hearing of a society that held an annual competition, Who could find most wild flowers, each flower not only to be seen but touched? 'I am sorry,' I said and made as though I would move away. 'Don't leave me,' she screamed, clutching my arm. We struggled down to where near the foot the chauffeur was waiting. 'Madam, is this the flower you are looking for?' he asked. He was pointing to a Cheddar Pink. She looked at the plant and she looked at me; then, having stooped and touched it, she took the chauffeur's arm and left me to follow behind.

13 Flowers

A flower might be called an inn-sign, if it were not itself the inn. It invites insects to call for refreshment, advertising its honey, or perhaps its pollen; for some attractive flowers, such as Roses, have no honey. Bees carry home pollen as well as honey, bearing it in hairy baskets on their legs, to knead into bread for their children. Other insects eat the fat and drink the sweet and fly away. For this refreshment the flower asks no payment; it only hopes the insect will not be too tidy at its meal, but smeared with the fertilizing pollen, the 'Father-Dust', convey it to another flower of the same kind. Mere pedestrians, such as ants, are not wanted, for pollen on their bodies is likely to be rubbed off on the grass and wasted; often hairs on the stem prevent their approach. The visits a flower welcomes are, so to speak, flying visits; moths do not even alight, but push their long tongues through the door. The entertainment, including the inn, is expensive for the plant; among annuals it is the usual cause of death.

Not all plants of course are pollinated by insects; the greater part, if not self-pollinating, are pollinated by the wind. Most forest trees are, as we might guess from their height; so too are the closely growing Rushes, and various Grasses, including cereals, gift of Ceres, goddess of corn. But wind-pollinated flowers as a rule are inconspicuous, often green and without scent or honey. Who sees the Wheat's flower, that opens for an hour or so very early on a sunny morning? We notice the Palm Willow's gold-dusted inflorescence, standing upright to attract insects, but not so often the Poplar's, hanging down for the wind to shake and empty of its pollen. A wind-pollinated flower is disregarded by most people; it is not

Digitalis purpurea.
Purple Foxe gloues.

That bridal bed the vulgar term a flower.[1]

Flowers, like young poets, attract attention to themselves by forming a group, as in the cyme of the Elder or the raceme of the Foxglove. The commonest kind of group is the compound umbel we see in the Hemlock's family; these umbelliferous plants are so successful that they number about sixty in this country, some of them rare no doubt, but others almost too plentiful, such as Fool's Parsley and Cow-parsnip. But their success is due, not only to the show they make, but even more perhaps to the ease with which they are pollinated, for flies, crawling about them, eager to lick up the honey, carry the pollen from flower to neighbouring flower. They attract flies more than the better class of insect; indeed, to ask a long-tongued butterfly to lick honey

1. Crabbe: 'The Parish Register'.

from the flat flowers would be like Aesop's fox asking the stork to eat soup from the shallow plate. They do not greatly attract us; yet we might in many cases admire their fernlike leaves. (Chervil, whose name seems to be Greek for Rejoicing in its Leaves, is not flattered by being called Honiton Lace.) Perhaps we do not admire them enough. Few people admire the Carrot; yet Parkinson says:

the beauty whereof allureth many Gentlewomen oftentimes to gather the leaves, and stick them in their hats or heads, or pin them on their arms in stead of feathers.

One wonders if this practice will become fashionable again. Even Parsley we use to garnish a dish rather than garland our heads. Yet Horace tells Phyllis he has not only a cask well filled with Alban wine, but Parsley in his garden for weaving wreaths. The Greeks used to dance to a popular song, called *The Flowers*:

Where are my roses, where are my violets, where is my pretty parsley?

Sometimes a large number of florets are crowded together in a head. A Clover is made up of florets, each a complete Pea-like flower; we see this better when the fertilized florets have withered and drooped, and the others remain upright, like the last survivors in a battle-field. The Compositae, the family that includes Daisy, Dandelion, Thistle and what not, are so called because their flower-heads are composed of florets, and they are not only much the largest family in the world, but the most advanced; botanists put them, so to speak, at the top of the tree. They too are readily pollinated, and in most cases have the further advantage of feathery fruits, that floating like ghosts on the wind disperse the seed. We see them in the Thistle's tousled head or the elaborately coiffured head of Goat's-beard, or of course the Dandelion's clock, from which children so carelessly blow away the hours. Sometimes the florets are strap-shaped as in the Dandelion, and sometimes tubular as in the Tansy. The Daisy comes between these, combining both kinds, strap-shaped florets forming the white fringe, thirty or so female flowers that are merely for show, and the tubular ones, two hundred or more, each a complete flower, massed together to form the yellow centre. A Daisy,

> the Danäe of flowers,
> With gold up-hoarded on its virgin lap,[2]

is a garden in itself; the gold in which Jove descends is flowers, and the virgin lap is flowers; never was there a more flowery wedding.

Flowers attract insects also by their colour; indeed the problem often is how to keep some of them away. Many insects, besides the pedestrians, are not desired by certain flowers; flies, for example, that flitting from one kind of flower to a different kind are likely to deliver the pollen at the wrong address. The problem is usually solved by the flower secreting its honey, perhaps in a tube, where it cannot be reached by their short tongues. Bees on the other hand are desirable insects, for they keep to much the same kind of flower in their flights; no doubt

> The singing masons building roofs of gold[3]

prefer a pure quality of honey; also it may save time. Many flowers appeal to them through their favourite colours, blue and purple. Probably the appeal is not to any artistic taste, but to their taste for food, the colour awaking the memory of a pleasant meal. If people seldom now grow Borage in their gardens to cool wine, they grow it for the sake of their hives. Yellow also attracts bees, as Violets know to their cost; though their love is all for bees, as we gather from their colour, shape and scent, they are deserted by them for the golden glory of the Palm Willow. Fortunately Violets produce strange summer blooms that pollinate themselves, not flowers

> sweeter than the lids of Juno's eyes
> Or Cytherea's breath,[4]

but green buds without honey or scent, blind eyes that never open. Butterflies are much less reliable than bees, flighty creatures, sipping from such a mixture of flowers, that one might imagine this is the reason they stagger as they fly. They appear, however, to show a liking for red. Certainly in spring, when few butterflies are about, there are few red flowers. Only Red

2. Beddoes: 'The Bride's Tragedy'.
3. *King Henry V.*
4. *The Winter's Tale.*

Campion is common, often in the company of Bluebells in a wood. (It is strangely absent from a few southern counties.) Its relation, Ragged Robin, is not uncommon in damp places, and one might wonder if there is a further attraction in its tattered dress. The Pinks, more distant relations, look pretty in their edge-cut petals, but Ragged Robin has carried that kind of effect much farther. Perhaps by cutting up its petals it makes itself more conspicuous without the cost of more material. We can hardly think that for butterflies and other insects, as for man, 'that noble insect',

> A sweet disorder in the dresse
> Kindles in cloathes a wantonnesse.[5]

Scents also to some extent attract insects. When the Queen of Sheba visited Solomon, she presented him, according to the Talmud, with two bouquets, and asked him to say which was natural and which was wax. Solomon, seeing a cluster of bees hanging on the window, had them brought in to decide the matter, and, as we may suppose, they decided it by the scent. Yet Solomon might have settled it himself, for bees are said to have no stronger sense of smell than we have; perhaps he was distracted by other scents, for we read, 'Neither was there any such spice as the queen of Sheba gave king Solomon'. Flies are drawn in scores by an unpleasant smell, and wasps, being carnivorous creatures like ourselves, by the meaty odour of a few flowers, such as Figwort; but fragrance seems to attract chiefly night-flying moths. The darkness that hides them from their enemies also hides the flowers in which they find their food. So flowers send out their invitations by scent; Honeysuckle, that strengthens its scent in the evening, can be detected by a Hawkmoth at a hundred yards. One wonders what happens on a gusty night, when the invitations are scattered about; moths must get impatient, like people going to a dance and continually having to ask their way. Flowers help them by showing, as it were, a lighted window, a colour not easily drowned in the dark, yellow or white. Evening Primrose, that opens so suddenly that it took Keats by surprise,

5. Herrick: 'Delight in Disorder'.

startled by the leap
of buds into ripe flowers,[6]

is called Primrose only because it is yellow.

Now sleeps the crimson petal, now the white –[7]

Tennyson has the right order, and long after we have lost sight of Red Campion, we can distinguish White Evening Campion glimmering through the dark. Night-flowering Catchfly, a pinkish slattern bud by day, opens in the evening white and scented, gleaming like Hero's torch that guided Leander across the Hellespont. One feels there is something dissipated about these flowers, but their gay life is short, a night or so at most.

That flowers nowadays are not so much grown for their scent seems clear from the case of Dame's Violet. Called by botanists Hesperis, Daughter of the Evening, because it reserves its scent till dusk, this was at one time a favourite flower in gardens, but now it is despised. A friend, introducing me to a Lecturer in Botany – the same who showed me the Twayblade – said, 'I will leave you two to have a talk'. Not knowing what to say in so embarrassing a situation, I said the first thing that came into my head, 'Do you happen to know where Dame's Violet grows?' 'Dame's Violet', he replied with a puzzled look, and then, 'Ah, you mean Hesperis matronalis. I cannot say I do, but I will try to find out'. He was better than his word, for next day he called for me in his car and we drove into the country. Stopping at the entrance to a large mansion, he said, 'We must ask permission to look for it'. I fancy our arrival was not unobserved, for while we were interviewing the lady who owned the place, a son and two daughters and several guests drifted into the room. To each in turn the purpose of our visit had to be explained. A tremendous discussion about the plant arose; if a gold-mine had been discovered in the grounds it could not have created greater interest. Though none of them knew anything about wild flowers, they all knew someone who did, and 'What a pity So-and-So is not here', they said. The son had the presence of mind to ring for sherry. The Lecturer, unaccustomed to discussions of

6. 'I Stood Tip-toe'.
7. 'The Princess'.

the kind, in fact I doubt if he knew what they were discussing, sat silent and bewildered; but wild flowers have made me familiar with most situations, and I joined in the conversation; unfortunately I conveyed the false impression that Dame's Violet was a flower of extraordinary rareness and beauty. Gratified by the interest that had been aroused, I rose at last and said, 'Perhaps we should go and look for it'. No one stirred, however, except the Lecturer. 'Have another glass of sherry to help you,' said the son; but, leaving them to carry on the conversation, we went out by a french window. When we found it in a few minutes, the Lecturer was for returning to the room, but I insisted we must kill time by walking about the grounds. 'Whatever for?' he asked. 'It will look better', I explained. When we did return with a Dame's Violet and showed it, they were visibly disappointed. The Lecturer made things worse by saying, 'It must have originally come from your garden'. 'So it is only a garden escape', they cried. As the son, however, thought the occasion demanded more sherry, I felt the incident passed off well enough.

14   A Confession

One year I thought I would go bird-watching; so I bought a pair of field-glasses, and with these slung over my shoulder I used to set off. I hoped my neighbours would think I was an ornithologist; what they thought was that I had taken to attending race-meetings. But as I had done nothing to suggest an interest in plants, I was surprised one day when a stranger called and said, 'I understand you are a botanist'. When I told him he was mistaken, he rose to go, but 'Sit down', I said, and we had a pleasant talk. He told me he was well over seventy, was unable to get about much, and would never again climb a mountain; could I – and here the object of his visit appeared – could I send him any plants for his herbarium? I was so touched by this appeal, that a few weeks later, climbing in the Highlands, I picked the very rare Snow Gentian. Wrapping it carefully in moss, and adding a few common flowers that I thought would remind him of the mountains, I sent it with a letter in which I said I hoped I was giving him a pleasant surprise. There was no doubt about the surprise, for he wrote back with strained politeness, thanking me for the common flowers, but saying nothing of the Snow Gentian. I knew what had happened; he had flung it away unnoticed with the moss. That's a lesson to me, I thought; I shall send no more plants to herbariums. How much lighter would be my conscience today, if I had kept to that wise decision!

A herbarium is a place, not where plants grow, but where they are buried, a collection of their dried unlovely corpses. Necessary for a botanist no doubt, to ordinary people it should be a shocking sight, like that Booth Museum of Birds at Brighton that Hudson, lover of birds, refused to view. But perhaps I am prejudiced. When Pepys visited Evelyn, in the interval between hearing part of a play or two of his making, very good, but not as he conceits them,

and hearing

some little poems of his own, that were not transcendent,

he was shown a herbarium, of which he says:

He showed me his Hortus Hyemalis; leaves laid up in a book of several plants kept dry, which preserve their colour, however, and look very finely, better than any Herball.

Sometimes wild flowers are collected, not to be put in a hortus siccus, as a herbarium is also curiously called, but to be grown in a garden. Many of them die, of course; they are like sea-birds that cannot be tamed; they have not the patience of the Aspidistra, content to exchange the dimness of an Asian forest for the dinginess of a cheap boarding-house. Even if they do survive, they look out of place. A garden is a kind of garden party, where everyone is dressed for the occasion. Most garden flowers have been doubled –

The Pink grew then as double as his Mind –

or crossed for colour –

And Flow'rs themselves were taught to paint.[1]

Wild flowers, that wear only their working clothes, are put to shame in such gay company. Yet where there is life, there is hope. I knew a Sussex botanist who excited the admiration, and indeed the envy, of other botanists by discovering all sorts of rare plants that none of them could find, Rosy Garlic, Bithynian Vetch, Naked Ladies and what not. They scoured the country in their cars, while he, poor man, walked. But that he found them all near Henfield, though the most mysterious thing about it, was also the explanation. The botanist Borrer had lived at Henfield and collected many rare plants in his garden; some had escaped, and now, a century later, their descendants survived in the neighbourhood. If Hudson could say

1. Marvell: 'The Mower Against Gardens'.

I confess that gardens in most cases affect me disagreeably; hence I avoid them,[2]

what must wild flowers feel in a garden? But as there is always a chance to escape, it is better to be alive in a garden than dead in a herbarium.

Worst of all of course is the habit of picking wild flowers for pleasure, maiming or destroying plants, and, for all we know, inflicting on them those palpitations and death-throes so painfully recorded by that ingenious Indian botanist, Sir Jagadis Chundar Bose. Against such a habit I might have hoped to quote the poets, but alas! they scoff at my sentimentality, if not by their words, by their practice. Wordsworth seems to weigh the matter in his mind when he speaks of

Nymphæa lutea.
Yellow water Lillie.

2. *Birds and Man.*

> some flower or water-weed, too fair
> Either to be divided from the place
> On which it grew, or to be left alone
> To its own beauty.[3]

We might have thought that one water-weed at least would have turned the scale, Water-lily, either the White that opens its petals, proud of being one of Nature's attempts at a double flower, or the Yellow that keeps them half-closed like a fist, as though it considered gold more precious than silver. For years Clare cast an acquisitive eye on some Water-lilies, and in the end, as he tells us, 'I brought the longest pole'. But we can forgive Clare; he wrote so much about wild flowers, perhaps more than all the other English poets put together. We can hardly imagine Cowper using a pole to draw in Water-lilies, but he tried his cane, and when that failed, his dog Beau plunged in and brought back a flower in his mouth. This became Beau's regular practice when they passed the place, and Cowper not only celebrated it in a poem, but wrote proudly to his friends, 'I must tell you a feat of my dog Beau'. People who own dogs, however, are not always quite sane. But what are we to think of Wordsworth? Nature, he says,

> early tutored me
> To look with feelings of fraternal love
> Upon the unassuming things that hold
> A silent station in this beauteous world;[4]

yet on an Evening Visit to the Lake what does the wicked wretch do?

> Rapaciously we gathered flowery spoils
> From land and water; lilies of each hue –
> Golden and white, that float upon the waves.[5]

But so far as Water-lilies are concerned, perhaps I am the last person who should cast a stone.

One day I went to Loch Lubnaig to look for that rare plant, Least Water-lily. I thought I saw it, but could not be sure that

3. *Poems on the Naming of Places*.
4. 'The Prelude'.
5. 'The Excursion'.

what I saw was not the common Yellow Water-lily. As it grew

In dangerous deeps, yet out of danger's way,[6]

I started to undress. A road runs by the loch-side, and on that summer afternoon cars kept passing up and down; but as I could not see the people in the cars, I imagined they could not see me. 'In any case it's their look-out', I said, perhaps more truthfully than I knew. I waded towards the plant and was standing waist-deep in water when I saw an open charabanc, full of holiday-makers, sailing down the road. I felt that was a different matter, and tearing off a flower I hurried back to the shore. My struggles to pull over wet shoulders a shirt that offered determined resistance were watched with interest from the approaching charabanc, and when just in time I succeeded, the hearty holiday-makers rose from their seats and, so to speak, 'greeted the unseen with a cheer'. Some people, I know, despise my methods of botanizing; yet few botanists have had their efforts publicly applauded.

Perhaps that Least Water-lily I picked lies too lightly on my conscience, almost as lightly as it floated on the loch, but it is not so with a more precious plant. I was staying at the railway station of Blair Atholl, not in the station itself, but in a railwayman's house that overlooked the line. The shining rails, that carried trains to the north, carried my thoughts to the Sow of Atholl, the one mountain home of Scottish Menziesia. My friend, Fordie Forrester, was staying at Blair Atholl too, and I reflected that he had a car that could take me to the mountain-foot. That he had no special interest in plants made me regard his mind as a kind of virgin soil in which to sow a passion to see Scottish Menziesia. Sure enough, I had not talked to him for ten minutes when I felt I had never known a keener botanist. 'But we shall not find it', I said; 'I am not sure it is not extinct'. 'Don't you worry; we shall find it', he replied; 'we start at ten o'clock tomorrow morning'. So next day we set off with our wives, Fordie wearing his kilt for the occasion. Everything looked bright and cheerful in the rain, Devil's-bit and Marsh Lousewort, the coloured patches of Sphag-num-moss, even the Cotton-grass in the black bogs, tossing their

6. Clare: 'Water-lilies'.

wool-tegged distaffs. A low mist halved the mountains; of the Sow itself only the lower parts were seen, its head wrapt in heavenly contemplation. 'Stop here', I cried at last, and getting out of the car we stood and viewed what was left of the mountain by the mist, which appeared to be always rising but never rose. 'We must spread out', I explained; so we began to climb in parallel lines that were soon lost in the grey darkness. For a time we wandered about, suddenly appearing to one another and disappearing, like the four lovers in *The Midsummer Night's Dream*. That I was the one to find the plant was not surprising, for I had received directions which I had not thought necessary to impart to the others. But having found it, how was I to find them? I kept calling till I began to think I had lost them for ever, and even Scottish Menziesia seemed scarcely to compensate for the loss. But one by one they loomed in sight. As we stood round the plant I remembered the old man who had thanked me sarcastically for the common flowers, but had missed the Snow Gentian. 'I will show him', I said, and I stooped and picked a flower. That night it lay in a glass of water by my bed-side, taking its last drink on earth. In the morning, resolved that this plant should not go astray, I wrote a letter to tell him what I was sending. Then, taking it from the glass, I looked at it; but as I looked, a sense of shame that I had picked it swept over me. I felt I had to get rid of it at once, and, stepping quickly to the open window, I flung it out. I watched it fall into an empty truck standing in the station. Wherever that truck went, it did not take with it the Scottish Menziesia, at least not altogether; it lies too heavy on my conscience.

15   The Morals of Plants

I

Tennyson, plucking a plant from a crannied wall and holding it, root and all, in his hand, said that if he could understand what it was he would be the complete philosopher. But was that a way for a poet to start a Contemplation Upon Flowers, to tear one up by the roots? And having done so, how could the monster address it by the term of endearment 'little flower'? In any case the incident had no importance (except for the plant); the poet had no hope of understanding it and becoming the complete philosopher.

Possibly the plant was Ivy-leaved Toadflax, called also Wandering Sailor and Mother-of-Thousands. These two names may seem contradictory, but they mean the same thing: the plant – it is an alien – has spread far and wide. Its success is partly due to an unusual gift: it can turn away from the sun. While still in flower, the flower-stalk bends towards the light, but when the seed is set, it turns from it, so that the seeds are dropped in a convenient cranny of the wall. Even though this remarkable gift were understood, should we be much nearer understanding what the plant is in itself?

When Jacob Boehme, falling into an ecstasy, went into the fields, he saw, not what we see, but the *very* herbs and grass:

> German Boehme never cared for plants
> Until it happed, a-walking in the fields,
> He noticed all at once that plants could speak,
> Nay, turned with loosened tongue to talk with him.[1]

1. Browning: 'Transcendentalism'.

But that kind of walk and conversation is rare. For most people there is a great gulf fixed between plants and ourselves; though we share the same earth, we belong to different worlds.

> Thus Nature shows the rose's paint;
> Us with the outside doth acquaint,
> But keeps reserv'd the soul of the fair plant.[2]

Plants of course bear some superficial resemblances to ourselves. When Wood Sorrel folds its leaves down at night and Clover folds them up, we say they go to sleep; yet it is not clear that they were ever awake. Some flowers, such as Elecampane, bow to the sun as though they were Zoroastrians; but that is only because the shaded side of the stem grows more quickly than the other. It is easy and tempting to attribute to plants our own habits and even sentiments, looking in a mirror rather than reading in a book. Maeterlinck is more dramatic in his botanical writings than in his plays:

> Though there be plants and flowers that are awkward or unlucky, there is none that is wholly devoid of wisdom and ingenuity. We can see that the flower sets man a prodigious example of insubmission, courage, perseverance and ingenuity.

Yet plants are not like ourselves. Lindley, himself called after a plant, his name meaning Lint or Flax Field, turned down the twigs of a young Willow till they rooted in the ground; then he pulled up the original roots so that the tree grew upside down. But when Marvell said,

> turn me but, and you shall see
> I was but an inverted Tree,[3]

no Lindley of the time took him at his word. When Godolphin lost his finger, he realized how unlike a tree he was:

> How much more blest are trees than men!
> Their boughs lopp'd off will grow again.[4]

Whatever plants are, they are not persons like ourselves. Perhaps

2. William Hammond: 'To Eugenio'.
3. 'Upon Appleton House'.
4. 'On the Loss of his Finger'.

they are higher beings, especially wild flowers; why else does Suso address the Eternal Wisdom,

> Ah! Thou tender delicious Wild Flower?

Whether plants feel pain or not is a different matter. It was disputed by the early Greek philosophers. Two of them thought they did, Empedocles and Anaxagoras. Empedocles ought to have known, having been a plant himself in a former life, as he says:

I was born once a boy, and a maiden, and a plant, and a bird, and a darting fish of the sea.

But his testimony has not seemed convincing, and we are no wiser yet. We can still say of a plant,

> If life taste sweet to it, if death
> Pain its soft petal, no man knows:
> Man has no sight or sense that saith.[5]

But while plants are not persons like ourselves, it has been the practice to imagine they were. What chapter in *The Anatomy of Melancholy* is more likely to have got Dr Johnson out of his bed two hours sooner than he wished to rise than that in which Burton tells of trees falling in Love? He gives an instance out of Florentius his Georgics of two palm-trees that loved most fervently:

You might see the two trees bend, and of their own accords stretch out their boughs to embrace and kiss each other.

He quotes Ammianus Marcellinus as saying that they marry one another, and fall in love if they grow in sight; and when the wind brings the smell to them they are marvellously affected:

If any man think this which I say to be a tale, let him read that story of two palm-trees in Italy, the male growing at Brundusium, the female at Otranto (related by Jovianus Pontanus in an excellent poem, sometimes tutor to Alphonsus junior, king of Naples, his secretary of state, and a great philosopher) which were barren, and so continued a long time, till they came to see one another growing up higher, though many stadiums asunder.

5. Swinburne: 'The Sundew'.

From poets we expect such things; even so, one wonders what Charles Darwin thought of Erasmus Darwin's *Botanical Garden*. Did he think his grandfather was drawing the long bow when he described how the plant called Impatiens shoots out its seeds?

> With fierce distracted eye IMPATIENS stands,
> Swells her pale cheeks, and brandishes her hands,
> With rage and hate the astonish'd grove alarms,
> And hurls her infants from her frantic arms.

This way of regarding plants has been called 'the pathetic fallacy' and 'the deadly sin of anthropomorphism'; even poets have frowned on it:

> brother Naddo shook
> The solemnest of brows: 'Beware', he said,
> 'Of setting up conceits in nature's stead!'[6]

Yet to this fallacious and sinful way I intend to keep. For all we know it may be better than the negative way in which some people regard them, as though they were not living beings at all:

> Yet if Astra pass the bush,
> Roses have been seen to blush —[7]

we may think such a statement goes too far, whatever Thyrsis thought; we do not know enough about Astra; but as Mrs Browning says,

> A tree's mere firewood, unless humanized.

She even advises poets to give plants a voice with human meaning; otherwise they will stand confessed

> Instructed poorly for interpreters,
> Thrown out by an easy cowslip in the text.[8]

As all my scholarship is in flowers – 'my fruits are only flowers' – I felt I must at any cost avoid such a catastrophe:

6. Browning: 'Sordello'.
7. W. Browne: 'Thyrsis' Praise of his Mistress'.
8. 'Aurora Leigh'.

And so I came to phansies medow strow'd
With many a flower.[9]

II

It would be only charitable to suppose that if plants have morals, they are much better than our own; and indeed for that we have good authority. 'Homo est planta inversa': 'Man is a plant standing on its head' – that ancient dictum suggests that in comparison our morals are shallow-rooted and paradoxical. Even a Bishop says,

> Brave flowers, that I could gallant it like you
> And be as little vaine,
> You come abroad, and make a harmless shew,
> And to your bedds of Earth againe;
> You are not proud, you know your birth
> For your Embroiderd garments are from Earth.[10]

No doubt St Francis preached to the flowers, but perhaps he was wiser when he provided a plot for them in his convent garden, 'that all who saw them might remember the Eternal Sweetness'.

Dr Johnson, making fun of Grainger's 'The Sugar-Cane, a poem', says,

> One might as well write, *The Cabbage-garden, a poem*;

but on further reflection he adds,

> One might say a good deal about cabbage. The poem might begin with the advantages of civilized society over a rude state, exemplified by the Scotch, who had no cabbages, till Oliver Cromwell's soldiers introduced them.

On which Boswell remarks,

> He seemed to be much diverted with the fertility of his own fancy.

Yet it was a Scotsman, Andrew Fairservice, who first pointed out the beauty of this wonderful plant: 'a kailblaid, or a colliflour,

9. George Herbert: 'The Pilgrimage'.
10. H. King: 'A Contemplation Upon Flowers'.

glances sae glegly by moonlight, – it's like a leddy in her diamonds'. But what we admire most in a Cabbage is its goodness. In its wild unreformed state, as it grows on the sea-cliffs of Kent or Cornwall, it is an ungainly, useless plant; but no plant has carried so far St Paul's great Christian injunction to be all things to all men. Sometimes, not afraid to make a fool of itself for others' good, it appears in our gardens as an enormous bud, the condition in which we usually call it a Cabbage. Sometimes it curls its outer leaves, and we call it a Savoy; sometimes it curls them more and also lengthens its stem, and we call it Curly Kale. When it develops a number of buds between the leaf-stalk and stem, the place where buds naturally grow, it gives us Brussels Sprouts. When it develops a large head of immature flowers, we have a Cauliflower or Broccoli; when it develops a swollen stem, we have Kohlrabi. People in Jersey, picking off the lower leaves, cause the stalk to grow a dozen feet or more, and this accommodating plant becomes a walking-stick. Is there such another plant in the world? Sir Anthony Ashley is credited with the introduction of the cultivated Cabbage into England – like many other vegetables it arrived in the sixteenth century – he lies in honoured effigy on his tomb at Wimborne St Giles, a helm at his head, a doubtful-looking Cabbage at his feet.

Other members of the Cabbage's family have done it credit. Black Mustard has given us a favourite condiment, though perhaps it does not compare with that Greek mustard, of which a Dining Philosopher in Athenaeus says, 'and when I had tasted it I wept that on the morrow I should not see it again'. White Mustard seldom lives to lose its first innocence, being eaten in tender infancy along with a foreign kind of Cress. Wild Navew, in giving us the Turnip, has done more to raise our standard of living than all the social reformers. Before Turnips came, farmers were unable to feed their cattle during winter and killed most of them off in autumn; now we can eat fresh meat throughout the year. More of course could be said for Turnips; when the bride of the fourth Lord Aberdeen came to Scotland about the beginning of last century, she was given Turnips as dessert, and, let us hope, she regarded them as a great delicacy. We should not be surprised when Lovelace says,

> Twas a blith prince exchang'd five thousand crowns
> For a fair turnip.[11]

He appears, however, to be mistaken about the vegetable, and also the price; it was a Radish and the price was a thousand crowns! A peasant called Connan, at whose cottage Louis XI rested when he went hunting, paid the king a visit, and on his wife's advice took with him Radishes.

> But as he went by the way, he yete up all the radyshes save one of the greattest. And the kynge toke it more gladly, and bad one, that was nearest to hym, to laye it up amonge those jewels that he best loved; and than commaunded to gyve hym a thousande crownes of golde for his radishe rote.

Not caring for the vegetable myself, I cannot say if a thousand crowns is a fair price for a Radish.

The name Swede, meaning Turnip from Sweden, reminds us that we cannot claim much of the credit for converting wild plants to vegetables. Most vegetables arrived from abroad during the Sixteenth Century. Cos Lettuce is called after the Island of Cos, where the Greeks had their first school of medicine, and Shallot after Ascalon, the Philistine seaport. Jerusalem Artichokes, however, do not come from Palestine, but from America; Jerusalem is Girasole or Sunflower, and suggests they were first welcomed by the Italians. Wild Beet, which is plentiful in many places by the sea, and has given us Beetroot, Sugar Beet and Mangold, appears to be named for some reason after Beta, second letter of the Greek alphabet. But what are we to think of our practice of eating these vegetables? When St Anthony of Padua preached to the fishes, he told them they were highly honoured in being used as human food; but the fishes, like other congregations, had no opportunity to reply. Are vegetables so simple-minded as to believe such a thing? They almost all come from the sea-coast, where salt gives them a natural succulence. Sea-kale grows on a shingly beach (not so dry deeper down) much as it does in a fat garden bed. Most of them are biennials, storing up food one year to flower and seed the next; they store it in some exaggerated organ, leaf or stem or tap-root. Sometimes, as though frightened, they bolt, shoot up and flower the first

11. 'On Sanazar's Being Honoured'.

year; it is not we who frighten them, but a drought, or perhaps a frost. Yet it is we who steal their food. That part of a plant we call a vegetable, Cabbage, Turnip or Radish, Ruskin very properly describes as its savings-bank. What credit does it do us to break into and rob a savings-bank?

That some fruit-bearing plants are even more virtuous than vegetables is suggested by Dr Boteler's remark about the Strawberry: 'Doubtless God could have made a better berry, but doubtless God never did'. But the plant is good in another way. In strawing or strewing the ground with runners, a common practice among plants, from which the Strawberry gets its name, it shows the same care for its offspring as an animal; through these runners it feeds the young plants till they are well established for themselves. Perhaps it is rewarded by seeing its children beget grandchildren, and these in turn great-grandchildren, the plant in fact becoming its own genealogical tree; but usually the gardener interferes.

Unfortunately we cannot claim as natives those famous plants, Green Pea, Broad Bean and Lentil, the last the least notable, though it has given its Latin name to the glass called a lens. Some of the proudest Roman families were called after Lentils, Beans and Peas, such as the Lentuli, Fabii and Pisones. Cicero was not ashamed to be called after the Chick-pea. Plutarch says he got his name from an ancestor who had a pimple on his nose, and when his friends wanted him to change it, 'he answered with great spirit, That he would make the name of Cicero glorious'. He also says that he dedicated in a temple a silver vessel inscribed with the names Marcus Tullius, followed by the picture of a Pea. The Green Pea was cultivated in the Stone Age, and it must be painful for so venerable a plant to be called by the ridiculous name Pea, a false singular of Pease, and also to be classed as a vegetable, when anyone can see its white flower, and the result of a flower is a fruit. The Bean was held in even greater honour, being regarded with awe by the ancients. Herodotus says the Egyptians never sowed Beans, as their priests could not endure the sight. Horace calls a Bean 'Pythagorae cognata', 'cousin of Pythagoras', attributing to that philosopher the belief that the souls of his ancestors had passed into Beans. There was a saying among the Pythagoreans, 'It is just as wrong for you to eat beans as to eat the heads of your parents'; and *The*

Greek Anthology tells that Pythagoras allowed himself to be killed rather than cross a Bean-field.

Alas! why did Pythagoras reverence beans so much and die together with his pupils? There was a field of beans, and in order to avoid trampling on them he let himself be killed on the road by the Agrigentines.

But after all, the most venerated plants were vegetables. It was a Mallow, a favourite vegetable with Horace, that Rhadamanthus gave Lucian, telling him to pray to it and it would guide him safely out of Hades. But more sacred still were the Onion and Leek.

Egypt chose an onion for its god,[12]

Porrum.
Leekes.

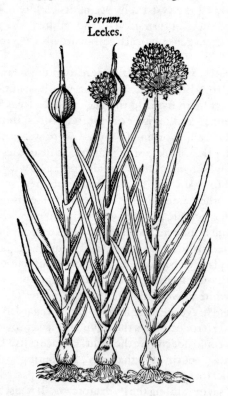

12. 'The Curse of Minerva'.

says Byron; and Juvenal cries,

> O sanctas gentes, quibus haec nascuntur in hortis
> Numina![13]

That people should think that gods grew in their gardens seemed shameful to George Herbert:

> Ah, what a thing is man devoid of grace,
> Adoring garlick with an humble face,
> Begging his food of that which he may eat,
> Starving the while he worshippeth his meat!

but mark what he adds:

> None will beleeve this now, though money be
> In us the same transplanted foolerie.[14]

The Onion is not a native, but we have the Leek, a plant that shared its divine honours. Some writers have treated it with contempt; 'not worth a leke' they say, and repeat the joke about an amorous old man being like a Leek, 'a hoor heid and green tayl'. But I respect the Leek as much as a Welshman does; in fact I reverence it more, regarding it as an Oracle that once proclaimed me a botanist. It may seem unlikely that I am, but as Socrates said when the Oracle at Delphi proclaimed him wise, 'I must believe the god'.

One day, walking about a Cornish town, I noticed a doctor's plate. 'No', I said and passed on; 'Yes', I said and came back. 'Is the doctor at home?' I asked, and the maid, inclining her head, ushered me into a room full of people. 'Good evening', I said, but though all looked at me, no one replied. That some were old, others infants in arms, made me conclude they had not come with the same object as myself. We sat in silence; then the door opened and the doctor appeared. Beckoning with his finger he said, 'Come along, Mrs —' at the same time giving me an inquisitive glance. I would have slipped away, but feared it might cast some reflection on the doctor and even on his patients. So I waited, feeling a grievance against the fate that compelled me to spend a summer evening in a doctor's consulting-room when I might have been surf-bathing on the beach. At last it was my

13. Satire XV.
14. 'The Church Militant'.

turn, and as I followed the doctor along a passage I was seized by a nervous apprehension. Good heavens! I must pretend some illness, I thought; but none of the illnesses I knew about, measles, mumps or erysipelas, seemed to fit the case. 'Well, sir, what can I do for you?' he asked. 'It's about –' I began, but the botanical name I had been carefully conning had vanished, and I could only add, 'the Leek'. A look of surprise came over his face, so I quickly explained, 'I mean the Wild Leek'. He stared at me thoughtfully, and 'I see' he said. Feeling that he was annoyed, I went on, 'I saw your name in the County Flora, and thought you could tell me where it grew'. Perhaps the mention of his name in the County Flora softened him, for when I left him a few minutes later I had the information. That same evening I took a bus and alighted at a river-bridge. It was already dark, and I had to grope my way cautiously along the bank. It was impossible to distinguish one plant from another, at least by sight, but fortunately I found the plant I wanted by its smell. Suddenly I recalled Wordsworth's definition of a botanist, 'a fine-nosed hound'. 'By the dog', I cried, the oath of Socrates leaping to my lips, 'the Leek proclaims me a botanist'; and, sure enough, the botanical name came back to me, Allium Ampeloprasum, confirming the Oracle of the Leek.

III

In his *Rêveries du Promeneur Solitaire* Rousseau tells of a walk he had with a companion, le sieur Bovier, along the river Iser. Tasting the fruit of Sea Buckthorn, he found it pleasant and went on eating while his companion neither ate himself nor said anything. A friend who met them exclaimed, 'What are you doing? Do you not know that fruit is poisonous?' 'Poisonous!' cried Rousseau in surprise. 'Without a doubt', he said; 'everyone knows it; no one in this neighbourhood would touch it'. Rousseau, turning to his companion, asked 'Why did you not tell me?' 'Ah! monsieur', replied le sieur Bovier respectfully, 'I did not dare to take that liberty'.

Though Rousseau was none the worse, when little George Borrow ate berries from a hedge, the red-coated dragoon, who had been chatting with his neglectful nurse, carried him home in strong convulsions. When Elisha's servant gathered a strange Gourd and seethed it in the pottage, the sons of the prophets cried, 'O man of God, there is death in the pot'; and when Antony's army ate an even stranger herb,

he that had eaten of it immediately lost all memory and knowledge, but at the same time busied himself in turning every stone he found, as though bent on important business.[15]

It may seem absurd to speak of such plants as having morals, and more absurd to suggest they are better than our own; but we shall see.

There are many poisonous plants among the Umbelliferae, especially among those that live in damp places, holding up white umbrellas as though they thought it was raining because their feet were wet. Cowbane is one of the worst, perhaps less dangerous to cows than to weak and inexperienced calves. If some of the Water-dropworts are poisonous, why do botanists call them by the attractive name Oenanthe, or Wine-flower? We are wiser ourselves when we call a poisonous plant of the hedges Fool's-parsley. But the most notorious is Hemlock, which having poisoned Socrates waits long for such another philosopher. Meanwhile it appears to keep its hand in by practising on asses, for Coles in *The Art of Simpling* says:

If Asses chance to feed much on *Hemlock*, they will fall so fast asleep, that they will seeme to be dead, in so much that some thinking them to be dead indeed, have flayed off their skins, yet after the *Hemlock* had done operating, they have stirred and wakened out of their sleep, to the griefe and amazement of the owners, and to the laughter of others.

But perhaps these plants are not so bad as they are painted. Parsley had an evil reputation once, not improved by the proverb, 'Welsh parsley is good physic', for by Welsh parsley was meant the gallows' rope. When Timoleon's army met some mules laden with Parsley, they were seized with panic; they recovered only when Timoleon made a speech and they all betook themselves to prayer and invocation of the gods. Some plants respond to good treatment. Celery, growing wild in ditches, is poisonous, but as

15. Plutarch.

it appears in our gardens, it is a reformed character; its blanching is no mere white-washing, as it checks the poison. Even of Hemlock it may be said that by its appearance, the port-wine stains on its blue-bloomed stem, it gives us a fair warning. Shelley, a kind of criminologist among plants, suggests they are often frank about their nature:

> All loathliest weeds began to grow,
> Whose coarse leaves were splashed with many a speck,
> Like the water-snake's belly and the toad's back.[16]

The Solanum family, which includes Deadly Nightshade, called by botanists Atropa, after the Fate who slit the thin-spun life of Lycidas, is more generally poisonous; yet to few families does mankind owe a greater debt. We should pity cannibals if they had no Cannibals' Nightshade to give a relish to their feasts. But we need not look so far afield; where should we be ourselves without the Solanum that gives our gardens one of its finest flowers, and also a useful vegetable? Sitting at table once I heard another guest exclaim to our hostess, 'What lovely flowers you have! What a charming decoration! What are they?' 'Potatoes', she replied. He might have seen much the same flower on Woody Nightshade, growing in any hedge. The Potato used to be called the Edible Nightshade. Though Gerard, in the frontispiece of his *Herbal*, holds the plant in his hand, the Potato was slow in getting known and used; 'What's this?' asks Bombo in Shirley's play, and Iacomo answers, 'Potatoe, bully'.[17] Puritans frowned on its introduction because it was not mentioned in the Bible; but Linnaeus frowned too, knowing it belonged to the Solanum tribe. The family poison asserts itself when a Potato, lying on the surface of the soil, turns green in the sun. The Tomato also was suspected at first, and considered only a garden ornament; as Dr John Hill says,

The plant is a kind of nightshade; we cultivate it in gardens. The Italians eat the fruit as we do cucumbers.

Few people nowadays would call the Potato a 'base root', as Cobbett does, or say with him,

16. 'The Sensitive Plant'.
17. *The Royal Master*.

It was one of the greatest villains upon earth (Sir Walter Raleigh), who (they say) first brought this root into England. He was beheaded at last![18]

Two members of the Solanum family, besides our own natives, grow wild with us, the Duke of Argyll's Tea-plant, and Thorn-apple. We should be ill-advised to make tea of the Tea-plant; its name is said to be due only to an exchange of labels, when along with a true Tea-plant, it was sent to the Duke. Probably the seeds of Thorn-apple came, and still come, as stowaways, perhaps in imported chicken-food, for it sometimes appears in gardens. It is a more poisonous plant; yet when I rid a garden of it once, my action was called in question. I had long kept a sharp look-out for this dangerous alien; then one day I detected it and, so to speak, ran it down. I was running from Par Harbour to catch a train, when I noticed from the corner of my eye a plant growing in a garden, where people sat round a table at tea. I recognized it as Thorn-apple and, without slackening my pace, sprang up some steps and seized it. A man in his shirt-sleeves rose from the table and shouted 'Hoi!' but I had not time to stop and explain I was ridding his garden of a poisonous weed.

Solanum comes from a word meaning to soothe; and sure enough, Tolstoy says people smoke Tobacco (a Solanum) to soothe their bad consciences. Thorn-apple is smoked for its soothing effect in cases of asthma. Henbane was a common narcotic in the Middle Ages. Dwale, another name for Deadly Nightshade, also meant a sleeping draught; in the Reeve's Tale, when the Miller and his wife went to bed, they had drunk so much ale, 'hem needede no dwale'. We can hardly think the monks of Furness Abbey used it to kill and not to cure the people who lived in the Vale of Deadly Nightshade. That members of this poisonous family should be used in medicine need not surprise us; medicamentum can be translated poison or remedy, for a small dose of poison may be a good medicine. How beneficent a family it is after all! It hardly needs the further light shed on it by Coles when he asks,

Why may not poysonous plants draw to them all the maligne juice and nourishment, that the other may be more pure and refined, as

18. *Rural Rides.*

well as Toads and other poysonous Serpents lick the venome from the Earth?

But when people think of immoral plants, they think rather of parasites. Originally a parasite meant merely one who sat at the same table. All plants in that sense are parasites, for all feed at the earth's table. But so crowded is this table that though we often speak of the earth, we seldom see it except in a ploughed field; and some plants have been tempted to prey on others. These are the true parasites, for a parasite came to mean one who sponged on other people, inviting himself to their tables. 'Parasite is now a disreputable term', says a Dining Philosopher; and another, to show how low human parasites can sink, adds, 'When a patron, after eating radishes, belches in their faces, the flatterers say he must have lunched on violets and roses'.

Our most familiar parasite is Mistletoe. Though it caused the death of the northern god, Balder, it belongs to a more or less tropical family. Pliny speaks of white-robed Druid priests cutting Mistletoe from Oaks with golden knives, but in only a few cases is it known to grow on our English Oak; perhaps the rind is too tough. It is not a pure parasite; that its leaves are green, though an unhealthy green, shows it does some work for its living; in fact it does not prey on the tree itself, but merely steals its food. Perhaps it is ashamed even of that, for it often grows downward, a peculiarity that suggested it was a cure for the falling sickness. That it should grow on a tree at all was so marvellous as to invest it with magic. It was to this Golden Bough, 'auro fulgentem ramum', that the goddess pointed Aeneas, bidding him pluck it that he might pass safely through the shades of Hades. To criticize such a plant is almost irreligious.

Who would suspect the pretty Eyebright of being a parasite? Yet it yielded to temptation and took to tapping the roots of other plants. No doubt there was a tendency to crime in the family, for other members have taken to the same practice, Bartsia, Cow-wheat, Yellow Rattle and Lousewort, sometimes called Red Rattle. They all have green leaves, though suspiciously small and dark; so theirs is only a case of petty theft. But we must dismiss them with a caution, for some of their relations have sunk into hopeless parasitism; if they were ever members of the family, they are now disowned, especially by its irreproach-able members, such as Foxglove and Snapdragon, and form a family by themselves, known as the Orobanchaceae or Vetch-stranglers. Toothwort, preying on the roots of trees, usually of Hazel, lives a subterranean life, little better than a Toadstool. The Toadstool appears above the ground as a fruit, Toothwort as a flower. It comes up to get married, so to speak, and presents a somewhat naked and blushing appearance. Its leaves are whitish scales, giving it the name Toothwort and a reputation for curing toothache. The other Orobanches are the Broomrapes, such hardened parasites that their seeds will germinate only in the presence of some plant on which they can prey – their host, as botanists pleasantly call it. As the chances of any particular seed falling in with such a plant are small, they produce an abundance of seed, and like the wicked of whom the Psalmist speaks, 'they are full of children'. They too are without green leaves, the working dress of honest plants.

The flowres without clothes live,[19]

says Vaughan, but compared with the naked Broomrapes most other flowers are well dressed.

Lesser Broomrape is common in fields of Clover, but it can live on other plants as well. Some Broomrapes, living on only one plant, or perhaps two, are rare. I had to visit a famous golf-course in Kent to find Clove-scented Broomrape. I found the players very unreasonable; when I walked across the fairway, they shouted and shook their fists, and when I crouched in a bunker, they thought I was waiting to steal their golf-balls. I met with a different kind of difficulty when I went to look for Red Broomrape, which grows on Thyme. I was walking on the cliff above Kynance Cove, when a man rushed up crying, 'Stop! they are going to shoot the Elephant Boy'. I saw a crowd on the beach, and was afraid for a moment the fatal deed was done; but, as it turned out, all he meant was that a film was being taken. I could distinguish the Elephant Boy, naked and brown as a Broomrape, seated on the sand, beating a small drum between his crossed legs. Evidently I was trespassing again, not in England this time, but in Africa. The man would not listen when I suggested the

19. 'Man'.

picture would be greatly improved by a distant view of myself, a lonely Englishman botanizing on the Atlas Mountains.

Broomrapes are not very harmful to their hosts, but with Dodder it is a different matter; its tangle of reddish stems can almost strangle a sturdy Gorse-bush. No one would take it to be a Convolvulus, unless he carefully examined the flowers. A Convolvulus, as the name implies, is a climbing plant, though Seaside Bindweed, finding nothing to climb, languishes like a sun-bather on the beach. Great Bindweed, climbing on other plants and saving its strength, produces large leaves and flowers, and is indeed a spectacular success; Dodder, inspired by a like ambition, became a climber too, but its climbing was the first step in its downfall. As the pretty Eyebright was tempted by the sight of so much grass, Dodder was lured by the closeness of the plant it embraced; but while Eyebright became nothing worse than a petty thief, Dodder grew to be a pure parasite, a vampire, a plant so degenerate that it has no roots except in infancy, no green leaves, nothing but a tangle of string-like stems, knotted with small waxy flowers. If plants are called to the Judgment, it will have to reply:

> I had Ambition, by which sin
> The angels fell;
> I climbed and, step by step, O Lord,
> Ascended into hell.[20]

To say that Broomrape and Dodder, pure parasites, have better morals than ourselves may seem paradoxical, but not if Lucian's defence of parasites, ironical for us, holds for them. Thinking somehow that it does, I am struck with admiration for Broomrape and Dodder.

At banquets, to go away with more than anybody else, enjoying greater favour than those who do not possess the same art – do you think that can be managed without some degree of theory and wisdom? The parasitic art comes by divine dispensation. It will appear pre-eminent among the other arts, like Nausicaa among her handmaidens.

But that parasites, and indeed all other plants, have better morals than ourselves, can best be proved by descending to what is

20. W. H. Davies: 'Ambition'.

usually considered the lowest class, the Insect-eaters, such as Sundew and Butterwort. If it can be shown that even their morals, doubtful as they are, put ours to shame, nothing more need be said.

These plants might plead that, living in poor boggy places and handicapped with weak shallow roots, they have turned to animal food only because nitrogen elsewhere was hard to come by; but even though the plea were not confusing cause and effect, have they any need to offer it to us? When we see a midge being slowly digested on the pale sticky leaf-rosette of Butterwort, our sympathy is with the midge, a creature we do not usually care for; yet all we are seeing is how our own stomach works. The plant is not ashamed of eating any more than we are. It holds up its beautiful blue flower, described with admirable inaccuracy as 'a violet springing from a starfish'; perhaps it is amused at its botanical name, Pinguicula, Little Fat One. But the offence in our eyes is that such plants invade our animal kingdom. Hemlock and Deadly Nightshade, Broomrape and Dodder, these never commit such a crime. Yet do we not invade their vegetable kingdom? And does that make us merely equal? Does it not make us much worse? They stop at small flies, but 'the hell-mouth of our belly' knows no bounds; we even eat that miracle of goodness, the Cabbage.

16   Poets' Botany

'My dearest Johnny', Cowper begins a letter, 'You talk of primroses that you pulled on Candlemas Day; but what think you of me who heard a nightingale on New Year's Day?' What was Johnny to think when the nightingale

> Sang in the Abyssinian vale
> That season of the year?

Was he to think his uncle had really heard it,

> As if the Abyssinian tree
> Had thrust a bough across the sea?[1]

Was he not rather to think he had been mistaken, being a poor naturalist? Fortunately a poet does not need to be a naturalist.

Certainly few poets have been botanists, though Simonides says,

> The poet dwells among flowers, like a bee busy with golden honey.

Gray kept two books on his table, Shakespeare and the *Systema Naturae* of Linnaeus, the latter so interleaved for notes as to double its size. Beattie must have had some perception of flowers to be the first to identify the small Two-leaved Linnaea. Crabbe wrote a flora of the Aldeburgh district, but was so browbeaten by a Cambridge don for writing it in English instead of Latin – an insult to science – that he flung it into the fire. His botanical studies were unprofitable in another way, for when he practised as a doctor, his patients, seeing him come home with handfuls of weeds, argued that as he got his medicines in the ditches, he could have little claim for payment. Lord de Tabley was competent to write *The Flora of Cheshire*, which still stands on botanists'

1. Ralph Hodgson: 'The Song of Honour'.

shelves. But these are exceptions. 'The Loves of the Plants' have not appealed to poets like their own loves; they would have agreed with Tennyson's Talking Oak that they were but 'vapid vegetable loves'. When Cowley and the Eyebright looked at each other,

> Thou only bard, said she, o' th' verdant Race.[2]

But perhaps we should say that poets have a botany of their own, which differs in some respects from the textbooks. When Herrick explains How Lillies came white or How Violets came blew, we accept his statement without further investigation. Only when he says that Primroses came green because they were Virgins troubled with Green-sickness, we raise a query, Are they green? But Spenser also speaks of 'primroses greene'. On the other hand John Hall says to Romira,

> And primroses white as thy fingers seek,[3]

making us wonder what Romira thought. There is no difficulty, however, about accepting Emily Dickinson's statement that bees from Clover

> Their hock and sherry draw;

botanists themselves speak of a flower's nectar rather than its honey, and the nectar the gods drank may have included both these wines.

Poets' Botany speaks of plants not referred to in textbooks, such as the Barnacle Tree. Mandeville told the inhabitants of Caldilhe about this tree, but found it hard to make them believe its fruits could change to birds.

> I tolde hem that in oure Contree weren Trees, that beren a Fruyt, that becomen Briddes fleeynge; and tho that fallen in the Water, lyven; and thei that fallen on the Erthe, dyen anon: and thei ben right gode to Mannes mete.

The birds born in this remarkable way were barnacle geese, and Irish priests are said to have eaten them on the ground that they were not animal food. There is nothing more remarkable

2. *Liber Plantarum.*
3. 'The Call'.

Anthyllis valentina Clusij.
Valentia Knot graſſe.

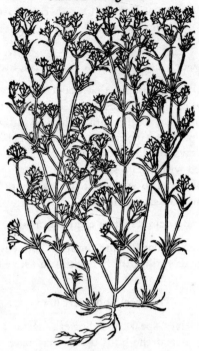

about this tree than about another tree of which Cleveland
speaks:

> A Scot, when from the gallow-tree got loose,
> Drops into Styx and turns a Solan goose.[4]

Yet if this seems fabulous, Darley insists there is nothing fabulous
about the tree he hails,

> O blest unfabled Incense Tree,
> That burns in glorious Araby,
> With red scent chalicing the air,
> Till earth-life grows Elysian there![5]

Poets' Botany differs from textbooks in the virtues it ascribes

4. 'The Rebel Scot'.
5. 'Nepenthe'.

to certain plants. Knotgrass is a poor plant, forming green patches on the ground; when Milton speaks of chewing flocks that make their supper of it, we feel the hungry sheep look up and are not fed. Yet it is fitter that sheep should eat it than children, for according to the poets it stunts their growth, and might be used for that purpose. So Lysander taunts Hermia about her height,

> Get you gone; you dwarf;
> You minimus, of hindering knotgrass made.

Burglars found it a blessing, as it kept a boy small enough to creep into a house; in 'The Coxcomb' Dorothy says to the Tinker,

> We want a boy extremely for this function,
> Kept under for a year with milk and knot-grass.[6]

In Knotgrass and a plant called Moonwort, which opened locks, a burglar had a complete outfit. This virtue in Knotgrass, if it can be called a virtue, was perhaps indicated by its habit of choking the growth of its neighbours. But to reduce a child's height was child's play compared with rendering a person invisible, the virtue attributed to Fern-seed. No doubt the explanation was that Fernseed was itself more or less invisible; for when a person carried about certain objects he had transferred to him their peculiar properties. Fern-seed must have seemed a godsend to highwaymen:

> We have the receipt of fern-seed, we walk invisible,

says Gadshill. It might have this virtue if there were such a thing, but ferns produce not seeds but spores. Yet the spores are almost as remarkable; for while seeds give rise to plants like their parents, spores give rise to quite different plants, and it is these that in their turn beget new Ferns. Ferns have, so to speak, no parents but only grandparents. Perhaps Falstaff himself was too fat to have much faith in Fern-seed, but he had faith in other plants, as when he wished the sky would rain Potatoes, hail Kissing-comfits, and snow Eringoes. The Potatoes were Sweet Potatoes, lately introduced into the country, the Kissing-comfits

6. Beaumont and Fletcher.

candied Plums, and the Eringoes the root-stocks of Eryngium or
Sea-holly, a plant not uncommon on our coasts. This Thistle-
like umbellifer, growing in sand, suffers almost as much from
drought as if it lived in the desert; but the roots run deep, and the
root-stock stores up water. The root-stock, prepared as a
confection, was sold in shops and served the same purpose as
Kissing-comfits. But the love-scenes, to which it was intended
to lead, must have been marred by unpleasant interludes, for the
name Eryngium means Causing to Eruct. ('To eruct, Sancho',
said Don Quixote, 'means to belch'.) Perhaps the more refined
Poins was aware of this, and ate conger and Fennel instead.

Poets of course refer to more ordinary uses of plants, especially
of fragrant garden herbs. These mostly come from hot dry lands,
where the scent is thought to cool the sun's rays as sprinkled
perfume cools a heated room. Napoleon on his way to Elba knew
in the dark he was passing his native Corsica, and Alexander the
Great, approaching in a ship, was first made aware of Arabia
Felix by scents borne on the wind. Even the names were fragrant.
Thyme creeps on dry hills – 'sunny thyme' Keats calls it; its
botanical name, serpyllum, is related to serpent; yet Milton,
merely enamoured of the name, imagines

> desert caves,
> With wild thyme and the gadding vine o'ergrown.[7]

No fragrance, however, is implied when Shrimp in Middleton's
The Family of Love says his master's hose are in lavender; he
speaks with the sarcastic humour of a poor boy of whom I asked
the time, and who beaming on me replied, 'Sorry, mister, I left
my watch on the grand piano'. Shrimp means that the hose are
in pawn. Rue had a bitter scent; 'O, you must wear your rue
with a difference'. But even so, Ophelia could pun on the name:
'we may call it herb of grace o' Sundays'; for there was another
word rue meaning repentance. Strangely enough Rosemary, Dew
of the Sea, had a double use; it was worn at both weddings and
funerals. Perhaps it was first used at funerals, and also in sick
rooms, as a guard against infection. A plant's scent may not only
keep it cool, but ward off noxious germs and insects. We adopt
a plant's own means of defence when we use Eucalyptus, Menthol

7. 'Lycidas'.

and Camphor. Rue and Southernwood (another plant of the south) were put in the prisoner's dock at the Old Bailey as a protection against jail-fever. But naturally a better explanation of Rosemary at funerals was given; so Ophelia says, 'There's rosemary, that's for remembrance'. Yet people for some reason also stuck Rosemary in their hats for a wedding. So Gnotho in Middleton's *The Old Law*, finding he has to bury one wife and marry another on the same day, the two events within half an hour – in fact he hopes to bury the old one on his way to the wedding – says, 'Besides, there will be charges saved too; the same rosemary that serves for the funeral will serve for the wedding'.

Poets' Botany has its own names for plants. If a textbook spoke of an elephant, some students might think it meant an animal, not a Scabious as in the ballad:

> the lilly leafe and the elephant
> Doth bud and spring with merry good-cheere.

Usually it is a simple country name, such as Kecks. Kecks are plants with hollow stems. Many plants, especially quick-growing plants that need to economize their material, have hollow stems. (Not trees, however, that store food in their trunks.) Hollow stems combine strength and lightness like the bones of birds. Strasburger considers that our highest and slenderest buildings, even tall factory chimneys, are extremely clumsy structures compared with Corn. But it is to umbelliferous plants, such as 'pipy hemlock', that poets give the name Kecks. Perhaps Clare thinks of Wild Beaked Parsley when he says,

> The ramping kecks in orchard gaps
> Shine like green neighbours in white caps.[8]

Yet sometimes a simple name may be deceptive; when old poets speak in admiration of the Daisy – 'Si douse est la Margarete' – they are often disguising a passion for their mistress. That, I suppose, is far from the practice of textbook writers.

Poets also have some peculiar ideas about plants. One is about Camomile, 'the more it is trodden on the faster it grows'; at least that was Falstaff's weighty opinion. If such a recovery seem

8. 'Evening'.

almost miraculous, it is not inconsistent with Camomile's reputation; it was called Plants' Physician, because set by a sickly
plant in a garden it helped it to get well. But perhaps all that
happens when Camomile is trodden on is that the crushed leaves
yield a stronger scent – of Apples no doubt, for Camomile means
Apple of the Ground. Another idea is that Corn can change into
weeds; so Donne says,

> Good seed degenerates, and oft obeyes
> The soyles disease, and into cockle strayes.[9]

Theophrastus thought it did, and so did Turner, 'father of
English botany':

Blewbottel groweth in ye corne, it hath a stalke full of corners. It
groweth much amonge Rye wherefore I thinke that good ry in an evell
and unseasonable yere doth go out of kinde in to this wede.

Modern textbooks, however, would reject such an explanation of
why 'thistles grow instead of wheat and cockles instead of barley'.
Yet another idea is that Water-lilies submerge themselves at
night. Sometimes the White dips slightly; Tennyson may be
excused for saying,

> Now folds the lily all her sweetness up,
> And slips into the bosom of the lake;[10]

but not Drummond, when he speaks of his love's hidden charms

> as a lily
> Sunk in the crystal's fair transparent belly.[11]

Though Water-lilies belong to a family called Nymphaea, their
flowers are not nymphs. They are careful to keep even their leaves
dry. With stalks growing at an angle, the leaves rise and float on
a flood, and their upper surface, through which they breathe, is
so coated with wax that water runs off like frightened drops of
quicksilver.

Poets regard the Red Poppy as a plant of sleep; but here they
come rather into conflict with the farmer, who must think it

9. 'To the Countesse of Bedford'.
10. 'The Princess'.
11. 'Song'.

too wideawake. Though so common, it probably wormed its way into this country in Corn-seed. It droops its flower-buds modestly, but when the petals open, coming crumpled from the sepal-sheath as though untidily packed, it defies the farmer, protected by his own ranks of Corn. Having no further use for sepals, this practical plant discards them. How different is the simple-minded Apple-blossom, that keeps its sepals so long that we see them as a withered crown on the top of the Apple! Most plants reward insects with honey, but the Poppy sees no need to offer more than pollen. As soon as the flower is fertilized, it discards its flaunting petals too, and, as though it thought religion would pay best in the end, it swings in the wind the perforated censer of its capsule. But no incense is jerked out to rise and assist the farmer's prayers; only a multitude of small black devils, seeds that hope as next year's Poppies to call forth his curses. Is this the plant that Virgil speaks of as 'steeped in Lethe's sleep'? Are the poets not harking back to One, older than Proserpine, *Mater Suspiriorum*, *Our Lady of Sighs*, of whom it is written:

> Her eyes, if they were ever seen, would be neither sweet nor subtle; no man could read their story; they would be found filled with perishing dreams, and with wrecks of forgotten delirium?[12]

The Opium Poppy was cultivated in Neolithic times. But what if poets do confuse the wideawake Red Poppy with the plant of sleep? If Mercury with his lyre could close the hundred eyes of Argus, Francis Thompson with his incantation can send the Red Poppy to sleep. He should know if it sleeps, and dreams in its sleep; Ovid metamorphosed other people into plants, but Francis Thompson did better, metamorphosing himself into a Poppy:

> I hang 'mid men my needless head,
> And my fruit is dreams, as theirs is bread:
> The goodly men and the sun-hazed sleeper
> Time shall reap, but after the reaper
> The world shall glean of me, me the sleeper.[13]

But poets can do what they like with flowers, even to making them flowers of speech. So Waller says,

12. De Quincey.
13. 'The Poppy'.

> Go, lovely Rose,
> Tell her that wastes her time and me . . .

No doubt it was a garden Rose he sent to his mistress, but if his purpose was to suggest the fleetingness of time, it was too long a sermon. He would have done better to send a Wild Rose, a more fugitive flower. A Wild Rose's life is two days, and the whole reign of hedgerow Roses, where White follows Red as the House of York the House of Lancaster, is over in four weeks. To see in the July dusk a White Rose glimmering like a moth is small comfort; it has set its seed, and is unconcerned to close and protect the pollen. It is the last Rose of summer. But in Wild Roses,

> Which in a blush their lives consume,[14]

no less than in longer-lived garden Roses, we may read something more than the fleetingness of time. As a child I read it first in a garden Rose. It was on the day I recovered my sight, having long lain blind with erysipelas, a disease sometimes called the rose; my father, returning from business, brought it as though to say,

> My love is like a red, red rose.

It was my first revelation of those eternal things, beauty and love.

14. Oldham: 'To the Memory of Mr Charles Morwent'.

17 Some Difficulties

One day I called on the rector of a Sussex village to inquire about a plant. I might have called on the doctor, but doctors in such a case are inclined to be supercilious. A parson usually gives me a welcome, thinking no doubt that, as the Apostle says, he may be entertaining an angel unawares; but unfortunately in the parson I am likely to draw a blank. This rector, however, an old man who might have spent most of his life in the parish, inspired me with confidence, and my hopes were raised higher when he assured me he took a great interest in the plants of the neighbourhood. 'Can you tell me where Euphorbia coralloides grows?' I asked. 'Where what grows?' he said. 'Coral-like Spurge', I explained. He looked at me sharply with 'That's not what you said'. As I sat silent, he went on, wagging his finger, 'Don't think an old man forgets all his Latin'. 'Or his Greek', I thought. For a moment or two he reflected, and then said, 'It does not grow about here'. 'But this is the only village in England where it does grow', I protested; but he shook his head. I told him that one of his predecessors, Manningham, had probably introduced it in the Eighteenth Century; 'he was a friend of Dillenius', I added to make it sound more convincing. Still he shook his head; 'He may have done so, but it does not grow here now', he replied. He was still shaking his head when I left him on the door-step to walk down the garden path and find the plant beside his gate.

I could not blame the old man for his blindness, having missed it myself on entering; and I have often failed to notice what was growing, so to speak, on my own door-step. When I lived in Midlothian I used to cycle down the Gala Water, searching the woods for a certain Wintergreen. (All that attractive name means is evergreen.) Then one day, chancing to enter a wood beside my house, I found it half full of the plant. Several summers I noticed a reddish flower in a neighbouring field, and 'Hemp Agrimony' I thought; then, walking into the field to speak to the farmer, I discovered it was the rare Willow-leaved Spiraea. My house stood by the Esk, but it was years after I left the district that I learnt that farther down the river grew Mountain Garlic. So I had to travel hundreds of miles by train to see a plant I might have seen by walking a few miles. I cannot claim credit, however, for having travelled so far only to see an Onion.

Rare plants as a rule grow in remoter places. Azalea, surprisingly enough, grows on the tops of Scottish mountains. Lecky said to Tennyson's son, 'Your father declared that he had persuaded one charming town-bred lady, to whom he was much attached, that a common daisy was a peculiar kind of Rhododendron only found in the Isle of Wight'. He might have found it almost as hard to persuade her that a small plant, creeping on mountain-tops, was an Azalea. The beautiful Andromeda on the other hand grows in marshes; it was for that reason Linnaeus gave it the name.

> The plant is always found on some little turfy hillock in the midst of swamps, as Andromeda herself was chained to a rock in the sea. Dragons and venomous serpents surrounded her, as toads and other reptiles frequent the abode of her vegetable resembler. As the distressed virgin cast down her blushing face through excessive affliction, so does this rosy-coloured flower hang down its head.[1]

(Botanists do not write like this nowadays.) But the only toad or other reptile the plant has to fear is the collector. Perhaps its namesake, the princess Andromeda, now changed to a constellation, guards it:

> Some kind herbs here, though low and far,
> Watch for and know their loving star.[2]

The Oyster-plant does not grow at Whitstable, but on northern shores where few feet tread the heavy shingle. Cycling one day on the west coast of Arran, I noticed from the corner of my eye a blue flower on the beach; 'Brooklime', I said, and cycled on. A mile or so along the road I jumped off, but with 'Don't be a fool; it was only Brooklime', I mounted again and continued my

1. *A Tour in Lapland.*
2. Vaughan: 'The Flower'.

journey. Two or three miles farther on I turned and cycled back to find the Oyster-plant or Seaside Smooth Gromwell. So I was late in arriving at Broadwaterfoot, where the minister had been expecting me to tea. When I told him the reason, explaining that wild flowers were my hobby, all he said was, 'What a disgusting habit!'

We are not likely to find many rare plants for ourselves, and are fortunate if we can get directions. Sitting one day by the cairn on Grasmoor, I took out my map to identify the surrounding mountains. I noticed a circle, drawn in pencil, round the summit of Grisedale Pike. At first I thought it was meant to mark a prehistoric camp, such as we see on the top of Caer Caradoc; then I suddenly remembered a botanist drawing a circle and saying 'That is the only place in England where Alpine Catchfly grows'. I sprang up and set off for Grisedale Pike. Passing Hobcarton Fells on the way, I was tempted to visit them instead; their lonely decayed rocks looked so attractive. I resisted the temptation, however, and pressed on to look for the plant. But I did not find it; as I learnt later, I had been misdirected, the plant growing, not on Grisedale Pike, but on Hobcarton Fells.

Even with good directions a plant may sometimes be difficult to find; it was only through losing my temper that I found Gladiolus. Any time I was in the New Forest I kept my eyes open for that rare flower, discovered about the middle of last century; luckily I kept my ears open as well. Staying in a Brockenhurst hotel, I overheard three men talking about beetles at breakfast; I thought to myself, Perhaps in their search for New Forest beetles they may have come across Gladiolus. So when two of them left the room, I approached the third, whom they had addressed as Lucas, and asked about a dragon-fly I had seen the day before. I could not have asked a better man, for, as I discovered afterwards, he was a great authority on dragon-flies; but at my insufficient description he shook his head. That of course did not matter; what I really wanted to ask was, 'By the way, have you ever come across Gladiolus?' 'Oh, yes,' he replied to that, and went on, 'Do you know the Rhododendron Drive?' I almost laughed; so many of my friends, who admire Rhodo-dendrons as much as I detest them, had asked the same question, adding, 'You ought to see it in June; it's a picture'. It was, in fact,

Chamædrys sylueſtris.
Wilde Germander.

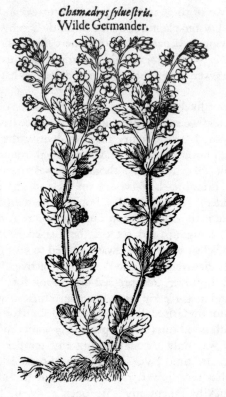

the one road in the New Forest that I had avoided. 'You take the
Rhododendron Drive', he said, and proceeded to give me
unmistakable directions. Later in the day, I marvelled at the sweet
temper in which I walked along the detestable drive. It was due
of course to the prospect of seeing Gladiolus. Yet when I arrived
at the place, my humour soon changed. The ground was covered
with bracken, under which, I supposed, the plant was hidden.
Wading through the thick growth I cried, 'Gladiolus, Little
Sword, where are you?' but the plant made no response. It was
only when I lost my temper and began slashing the bracken with
my stick, that the unwilling gladiator made his appearance.

Some difficulty may arise when a plant grows in private
ground, but that of course we might expect. Yet I was surprised
when, on my crossing a North Devon golf-course to find Water

Germander, the players protested, saying I was trespassing. That to me! who, having given up the game before I left school, regard myself as an honorary member of all golf-clubs. On another occasion I again felt aggrieved. I arrived one afternoon at a castle in a southern county to look for Wall Germander. More familiar with northern castles, I had imagined it would be a ruin, but found instead curtains waving from the windows. As I did not feel they were waving a welcome, I paused to consider the situation. To set the castle bell clanging for the sake of a wild flower seemed ridiculous, and it was far from my wish to disturb the household; so I started to climb the wall. An angry voice from above demanded who I was and what I was doing. It was then I felt aggrieved; its owner did not appear to realize that I was risking my life at the moment, or to appreciate that in climbing the wall without having clanged the bell, I was acting out of consideration for him. As I had just caught sight of the plant, I did not stay to explain and put him right. With Cut-leaved Germander I expected trouble; I had been warned that the Surrey farmer in whose ground it grew had a great hostility towards botanists. Finding his fences thickly knotted with barbed wire, perhaps a protection against holiday-makers from Box Hill, I decided my best course was to open the gate and walk up the drive to the house. There was, indeed, a notice to trespassers, but this did not seem like trespassing; on the contrary, I felt it had an air of frankness. I passed the house safely, but only to view with apprehension a man working in a field. I hoped he would be a labourer, but when, catching sight of me, he charged down like a wild bull, I knew he was the farmer himself. I hastened towards him and to his 'What do you want?' explained I was a botanist. 'I know you are, and I don't want any botanists here', he shouted. 'I am sorry', I said; 'are you much troubled with botanists?' That started him off; in the strongest language he raged at botanists, who knew they had no right to come on his farm and yet came. I tried to look sympathetic and kept repeating, 'I promise not to come again'. That he was seeing the last of me seemed somehow to pacify him, for 'all right; go on', he growled, and turned away. I have kept my promise; in any case why should I want to see Cut-leaved Germander twice?

Often an interesting alien appears in a garden, introduced in flower-seed or in some other way. Small-flowered Balsam is a common weed in Oxford gardens; one might imagine it had been banished to that city from its native Siberia. Usually the householder is glad to show any such plant; it gives him the opportunity of taking a stranger round his garden, though he regretfully explains his flowers are not at their best, as it happens to be what he calls 'between-times'. But a difficulty may arise. One day a botanist sent me a postcard with 'Amaranthus Blitum has turned up in the back-garden of 27 — Road, Southwick'. I was excited, for to see

> Immortal Amarant, a flower that once
> In Paradise, fast by the Tree of Life,
> Began to bloom,[3]

seemed like a foretaste of heaven. Yet when I looked up its picture in Sowerby, Amaranth appeared to be a miserable plant, much like a Goosefoot. I went, however, to Southwick, and found the house, a semi-detached villa. Drawn curtains told me its occupants were away from home, so I applied at the adjoining house. An unpleasant woman opened the door, and behind her stood her husband, in his shirt-sleeves, smoking a pipe. When I explained what I wanted, she did not seem to understand my request; yet it was simple enough, that I might stand in her back-garden and look over the fence into her neighbours' back-garden. She asked me such questions as, Did I know the people next door? Then why did I want to look into their back-garden? What was the flower I wanted to see? When I said it was Amaranth, she turned to her husband and asked if he had seen it; but he shook his head. 'What is it like?' she persisted. 'It's like – well, it's like a Goosefoot', I replied. Perhaps they thought I said 'goose's foot', for she looked significantly at her husband, and he, taking his pipe from his mouth, gaped at me in surprise. No doubt Professors of Botany explain to their students how to deal with such a situation, but I found it difficult. Yet the bees that put honey on Pindar's lips to give him a singing-mouth, may have put a drop on mine to give me a persuasive tongue, for in the end they took me into their back-garden. As we stared at the plant over the fence, 'What did you call it?' asked the husband. Excited

3. *Paradise Lost.*

at having gained my point, 'Amaranth', I cried, thrilled by the heavenly name. But his shirt-sleeves did not change to angel's wings; he merely puffed at his pipe. Yet they were extraordinarily nice people, inviting me to come again if I wanted to see any other flower.

That there should be any objection to seeking a plant on one's own property may seem unimaginable; yet such was my experience. The botanist who told me about Amaranth also told me that Purple Toadflax was growing on Hove dustheap. (How he discovered these things I have no notion.) Though I was not attracted to the place, Hove was where I lived, and I was unwilling to miss so rare and beautiful a plant. At the entrance I found myself confronted with the notice 'Trespassers will be prosecuted'. Familiar as I am with notices of the kind, this was something new; a rate-payer, I was forbidden to visit my own dustheap. Fortunately there was another notice, 'On business only', and as I conceived I was on business – who indeed would visit such a place for pleasure? – I opened the gate. I had not gone far when a man rushed forward and demanded what I wanted. Without stopping I stared at him coldly and said, 'I am a friend of the Borough Surveyor'. He hung about, watching me with suspicion, while I noted Flixweed, a cure for the bloody flux, Hungarian Mustard, an alien, and the plant I had come to see, Purple Toadflax. He was approaching me again, when I turned to walk back to the gate. It was not a place where I was tempted to linger. 'Well, sir, what did you want?' he asked; and though I passed him with a wave of my hand, it was what I asked myself. I cursed the day I had taken so unnatural an interest in wild flowers, that I could seek this beautiful plant on a dustheap. As the minister said, 'What a disgusting habit!'

18 Plants and People

Plants continually remind us of people. When we see an Appletree in a hedge, we think of someone who walked that road eating an Apple and flung away the core; now it stands as his strange memorial, that spring never fails to crown with flowers. A bush of Balm marks the site of a vanished garden; long after those

Nummularia minor.
Small Money woort.

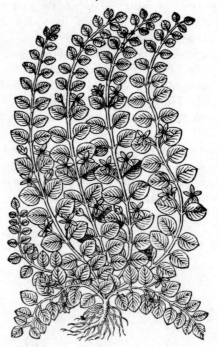

who planted it have gone, it still smells sweet and blossoms in their dust. Or Greater Periwinkle tells a tale:

> Here once the walls
> Of a ruined cottage stood.
> The periwinkle crawls
> With flowers in its hair into the wood.[1]

Perhaps it is not so much of people that plants remind us as of a human interest. Seed-pods and leaves are described as purses and pence, so that even in plants we may behold our natural face as in a glass. Wall Pennywort, that plasters walls in the West, and Marsh Pennywort, abundant in bogs, are named from their round leaves. Of Moneywort, better known as Creeping Jenny, Turner says,

> It maye be called in englishe Herbe ij. pence or two penegrasse because it hath two and two leaves standyng together on each syde of the stalke lyke pence.

Penny-cress on the other hand is named from its seed-pods, which are large, though not so exaggerated as those of its garden relation, called Honesty because they are transparent. The seed-pods of Shepherd's-purse are small:

> and therefore it was so called with grim and truthful humour,

thinks Richard Jefferies. But more often plants reflect an interest in animals. Foxglove is wrongly thought to mean glove of the folk or fairies; we must not let those beings steal the fox's purple gloves. Hound's-tongue has soft smooth leaves; but so far from giving tongue itself, it is said to keep dogs from barking; Cat's-ear is the commonest of those flowers that look like small Dandelions. Mice were evidently not frightened by such names, for no name is more frequent than Mouse-ear, as in Mouse-ear Chickweed. One gathers that a mouse's ears are soft and hairy. Some names are strange chimeras; in Viper's Bugloss we imagine an adder with an ox's tongue. Cranesbill and Storksbill have long beaked fruits, though all they peck at is the empty wind. Mare's-tail got its name in an odd way. Horsetail is the green plant that looks like a horse's upturned tail. It is of a type too ancient to

1. Edward Thomas.

have flowers, being a dwarf relic of those tree-like plants which soaked in the sunlight now imprisoned in coal. (Was there no coal in the Grand Academy of Lagado that the scientist spent eight years trying to extract sunbeams from Cucumbers?[2]) As Mare's-tail, a more modern flowering plant of ditches, somewhat resembles it, they were thought to be, so to speak, husband and wife; and as one was called Horsetail, the other became known as Mare's-tail.

A plant may even remind us of the jokes people enjoyed. One great joke was that the Aspen's leaves were like women's tongues, 'which seldom cease wagging'. In *A Hundred Mery Talys* we read of a man who married a woman, rich and beautiful, but dumb. To one who saw him right pensive and sad he explained the reason, and was advised to lay an Aspen leaf under her tongue while she slept. He was foolhardy enough to lay three, and in the morning when he demanded how she did,

sodenly she answered and sayd: I beshrowe your harte for wakenynge me so erly; and so by the virtue of that medycyne she was restored to her speche. But in conclusyon her speche so encreased day by day, and she was so curste of condycyon, that every daye she brauled and chydde with her husbande so moche, that at the laste he was more vexed, and hadde moche more trouble and disease with her shrewde wordes, than he hadde before.

Meeting the man who gave the advice, he asked what could be done; but the man, now frankly admitting he was a devil, replied:

All be it yet I have power to make a woman to speke, but and if a woman begyn once to speke, I, nor all the devyls in hell that have more power, be nat able to make a woman to be styll, nor to cause her to leave her spekynge.

Plants remind us of the uses to which they were put; people crumbled the dry leaves of Sneezewort to make snuff, and rubbed the oily leaves of Soapwort in water to wash their faces. Sweet Flag, strewn on a floor, sweetened the room with the scent of Apples and Lemons; of Meadow-sweet, sometimes appropriately called Bridewort, Parkinson says:

2. *Gulliver's Travels.*

Queen *Elizabeth*, of famous memory, did more desire it than any sweete herbe to strew her chambers withall.

Woodruff, put in a clothes-chest, grew fragrant as it withered, like the bodies of saints that smell of flowers when their coffins are opened. Loosestrife put an end to strife between restive oxen; so Pliny reports, but in *The Faithful Shepherdess* it is only said

> to give sweet rest
> To the faint shepherd, killing, where it comes,
> All busy gnats, and every fly that hums.[3]

(Yellow Loosestrife, not Purple, is the true Loosestrife; both grow by streams, but they have no connexion; they are like two unrelated families called Makepeace, living in the same street.) Teazel's use is more up to date; it is still employed to tease or raise the nap of woollen cloth, nothing better than its bristly flower-heads having been invented. Three plants used in dyeing were Dyer's Rocket, a tall Mignonette that shoots up to bend over like a rocket tiring in the sky; Dyer's Greenwood, probably the Broom called Planta genista that gave its name to the House of Plantagenet; and the famous Dyer's Woad, with which, as the poet Dyer says,

> our naked ancestors obscur'd
> Their hardy limbs, inwrought with mystic forms,
> Like Egypt's obelisks.[4]

As Woad gave its Celtic name to Glastonbury, no doubt it was much used. Fuller, following the observant Caesar, says,

> This woad gave the Britons a deep black tincture, as if they would blow up their enemies with their sulphureous countenances.[5]

It is thought to be native only on the river-bank at Tewkesbury; but it can be seen in a wild state in Guildford, living dangerously on a great chalk-quarry, that seems about to swallow half the town.

Of course the main use of plants was as medicines; even George Herbert reminds us:

3. Beaumont and Fletcher.
4. 'The Fleece'.
5. *The Worthies of England*.

A rose, besides his beautie, is a cure.[6]

In fact, if on a country walk, we were to consider too curiously the names and uses of plants we might as well be in a hospital, or even a maternity home. Rachel, in her desire to have a child, said to Leah, 'Give me, I pray thee, of thy son's mandrakes'. We have no Mandrakes in this country, but we have a plant with a peculiarly large root, Black Bryony. (Its dark bronze leaves distinguish it from White Bryony; it is our only representative of the tropical Yam family, as the White is our only Cucumber.) Gerard says:

> The Queenes Surgion Mr *William Goderous*, a very curious and learned gentleman, showed me a root hereof, that waied halfe an hundred weight, and of the bignesse of a child, of a yeare old.

The roots, carved in the likeness of a man, were sold to childless women as Mandrakes. For a childbirth the most famous herb was Mugwort. Who would think this dull plant, called Mugwort because it frightens away midges, had the botanical name, Artemisia, after Artemis, the Moon-goddess? Callimachus, setting little Artemis on the knee of her father Zeus, makes her say:

> On the mountains will I dwell, and the cities of men I will visit only when women, vexed with the sharp pains of childbirth, call me to their aid.

In Christian times her place was taken by one or other of the St Margarets, usually St Margaret of Antioch, who in *The Golden Legend* prays at her martyrdom:

> If any woman at child-travailling call on me, let her be delivered of the child.

Mugwort was the herb of Artemis, but St Margaret made use of the Moon-daisy, sometimes called Marguerite, a name that originally meant a pearl.

Plants, having brought a child into the world, did not fail it from cradle to grave. Nipplewort helped the mother to feed him, until like Juliet's nurse she weaned him with Wormwood. No childish complaint was without its cure. Of Thorough-wax, so

6. 'Providence'.

named because the stem waxes or grows through the leaves,
Culpeper says:

It being applied with a little flour and wax to children's navels that
stick forth, it helpeth them.

Golden Rod, or Solidago, Plant that Consolidates, could heal a
cut or wound. Gerard says the imported herb was sold in London
for half-a-crown an ounce, till it was discovered growing at
Hampstead, when no one would give half-a-crown for a hun-
dredweight:

This verifieth our English proverbe, Far fetcht and deare bought are
best for Ladies.

Feverfew means a plant that frightens away fever, and Angelica
was so named because, like the angel that hovered over the
threshing-floor of Araunah the Jebusite, it could stay the plague.
Devil's-bit, a Scabious with an oddly shaped root, gets its name
from the Devil's attempting to destroy so virtuous a plant by
biting the root. When we grow old, we may suffer from gout;
how foolish then to struggle, probably in vain, to eradicate
Goutweed from our garden! Its other name, Bishopweed, slyly
suggests what persons are most liable to gout. So there was no
lack of cures till one reached a dropsical old age. Even here
Apollo had several strings to his bow. Cowley, who gathered
simples in Kent with a view to becoming a doctor, strains his
imagination to describe the various cures for dropsy. Betony of
course was one, for there was nothing Betony could not cure.
Said to be named after a Spanish tribe, the Vettones, Betony was
introduced to Rome by Antonius Musa, Horace's doctor, to
whom an extant treatise on the herb is attributed. Cowley lets it
speak for itself:

> *Dropsies* like *Watersnakes,*
> With liquid Aliment no longer fed,
> By me are forc'd to fly their wat'ry Bed.

For Wormwood he claims a similar power:

> The Dutchmen with less skill their Country drain,
> And turn the Course of Water back again.

There is Fennel also, which he compares to a Water-goddess:

> It bids the Waters pass, the frighted Waters fly.

But best of all is Iris. Iris means Rainbow, the flowers appearing in various colours. If Noah's rainbow could promise no deluge again on the earth, this Rainbow could do no less:

> I am that Bow, in poor Hydroptick Man,
> The same refreshing Hopes contain,
> And when within him I appear,
> He needs no Deluge from the Dropsy fear.[7]

Plants gave their service to the end; as **Jeremy Taylor** says in *Holy Dying*:

> The spring brings flowers to strew our hearse, and the summer gives green turf and brambles to bind upon our graves.

Plants remind us more definitely of people, perhaps of our self. When Newman saw for the last time the Snapdragon on the walls of Trinity, it reminded him of the self he was leaving behind in Oxford:

> I had for many years taken it as an emblem of my own perpetual residence even unto death in my University.

Many plants remind us of our childhood and youth, though at the cost of emphasizing our age. Lily of the Valley, perhaps remembered only in a garden, though white flowers and scent are more adapted to a wood's dim stillness, droops as if with the weight of memories not its own. I have never heard the Elder called Boretree as in northern ballads, but I knew as a boy its pithy stems could be bored and used for shooting peas at passers-by from behind a hedge, suggesting that for once Providence was on the side of boys. Walking in a field, I find myself from force of old habit looking for a Four-leaved Clover, an amulet as lucky as White Heather. Clover is the picture on the playing-card now called Clubs – the French keep the original name – how lucky it would be in a game of bridge to find a Four-leaved Clover! Probably we recognize in Stinging Nettle our oldest enemy; probably too we feel no friendlier now, having never met it as

7. *Liber Plantarum.*

food on a table, or even as the table-cloth. Yet Nettles can be used as food; they are the only food of some caterpillars. The Nettle porridge Pepys ate at W. Symon's he said was very good, and Andrew Fairservice says they forced Nettles for their spring Kale in his parish of Dreep-daily, near Glasgow. When Nettles grow tough – stringy, as we say – the fibre that supports their tall slender growth can be put to the same use as the fibre of Flax. So the poet Campbell writes:

> I have slept in nettle-sheets, and I have dined off a nettle-tablecloth. I have heard my mother say, that she thought nettle-cloth more durable than any other species of linen.[8]

Plants remind us also of other people. 'Ah! voilà de la pervenche!' cried Rousseau with joy; he remembered how, nearly thirty years before, on the way to their new home, Madame de Warens had pointed out a Periwinkle. He must have been shortsighted indeed, for he had not noticed in the long interval those blue twisted stars. Spanish Catchfly reminds me of an innkeeper's wife. Having gone one afternoon to Mildenhall to find the plant, I was running to catch my last train. The road went past an inn, but foolishly I did not follow its good example. Hot and thirsty I entered, and rapping on the counter, called for a glass of beer. The woman, serving some countrymen, paid no attention. I cried that I had a last train to catch, but unaffected by my impatience she even took time to call through a door, 'John', and again 'John', with something about putting on his coat. Gulping down the beer, which, I reflected, was likely to cost me the price of a night's lodging in an hotel, I started again to run; but the race was now hopeless. Angry with the woman – not with myself – I was walking slowly along the road, when a car drew up and someone said, 'Jump in'. It was John, who had put on his coat.

Motherwort reminds me of a cabman so much that he haunts me, following me with his eyes like a portrait on a wall. I had gone into Barnstaple Museum – hardly a Temple of the Muses – and was looking with distaste at a ticketed collection of wild flowers, when a plant caught my eye, making me hasten to the curator's room. 'Motherwort?' he said; 'I think I can show you

8. *Letters from the South.*

the man who brought it'; and leading me to the entrance, he pointed out a cabman standing by his horse-cab. 'He's quite a botanist', he explained; he might have added that he carried about his own flora, for his hat and coat were green with vegetable mould. We had attracted his attention and 'Cab, sir?' he cried. Shaking my head I crossed over and said, 'It's about the Motherwort'. An ostler of the Crown Inn at Alton gave Curtis his first lessons in botany; it might have been this cabman. He told me where Motherwort grew, in a village a few miles away. As we stood talking of other plants, it occurred to me that I could catch a train to the village; so I thanked him and walked over to the station entrance. How often as a boy I had ridden in horse-cabs through Edinburgh streets, not sitting inside, but perched on the back axle, journeys which usually ended with a chase by a policeman! What devilish pride now made me ashamed of being seen travelling in so old-fashioned a conveyance? Having noticed his disappointed look when I turned from him, I felt he followed me with his eyes, the eyes, not of a botanist, but of a cabman in an old green hat and coat.

So plants remind us of people, both the quick and the dead. But what of that *tertium quid*, a ghost? When Sibylla in *Death's Jest-book* says that flowers

> Rise yearly from the neighbourhood of the dead,
> To show us how far fairer and more lovely
> Their world is,

she adds,

>   'tis the time of spirits,
> Who with the flowers, and like them, leave their graves.[9]

But only once have I thought of a flower and a ghost together. Wandering in an Angus glen, I was surprised to come on a footprint on a patch of sand. It pointed up the mountain, and looked so meaningless that I felt it had a meaning. I started to climb; several times I stopped to think how foolish I was, but each time went on, as though kicked by that footprint on the sand. Strangely enough, on perhaps the only rock in Great Britain where it grows, I found Yellow Mountain Oxytropis.

9. Beddoes.

That the footprint had been left by a botanist, I did not doubt;
yet in that lonely glen, so lonely that I felt no one had been there
before, it looked like the footprint of a ghost. I wanted to think
it was, encouraging the hope that I too might revisit the earth as
a ghost. And why not? Even now there are one or two woods
with which I have so mingled myself, that surely anyone walking
there must feel them haunted. Returning after an absence I have
felt they were, and it was I who haunted them, a *doppelgänger*, so
that I have said:

> O foolish birds, be dumb;
> And you, jay, stop your mocking laughter;
> A revenant I come
> Today, as I may come fifty years after.

Certainly I shall be sorry to bid this earth good-bye. If the old
custom of binding Brambles and Briars on graves was designed,
not to ward cattle off, but to keep ghosts down, let no one bind
them on my grave. But perhaps I shall find something better to
do than revisit the earth. I might search for plants I have not
found, that Moly – 'hard for mortal men to dig' – that saved
Odysseus from the snares of Circe, and that Nepenthe that made
Telemachus forgetful of every sorrow. I might even study botany.

19 Eve and Linnaeus

Milton tells us that when Adam had named the animals, he left it to Eve to name the plants, Eve who was to prove so poor a botanist at the Forbidden Tree, not discerning the nature of its fruit. Thomson considered it

> beyond the power
> Of botanist to number up their tribes,[1]

but Eve seems to have attempted some rough classification of plants, for Milton also says that in departing from Paradise Lost she sighed,

> O flowers, who now shall rank your tribes?

Certainly she could not have done worse than the Peripatetic philosopher who, in *De Plantis*, classifies them as Indoor, Garden, and Wild. But how did she decide on their names? Perhaps she thought like Sir Thomas Browne

> that there is a Phytognomy, or Physiognomy, not only of Men but of Plants and Vegetables; and in every one of them some outward figures which hang as signs or bushes of their inward forms. By this Alphabet *Adam* assigned to every creature a name peculiar to its nature.[2]

If the name that Achilles assumed when he hid himself among women is not beyond all conjecture, the names are, that were given at that Garden of Eden christening. Yet there is a sense in which Eve's names might be said to remain, that is, in the popular names of our mother tongue.

Linnaeus is Eve's great rival; and Adam's too; indeed one of his critics spoke of him as aping Adam in giving names to

1. 'The Seasons'.
2. *Religio Medici*.

animals. He had not, of course, Eve's task of inventing names; he used names already given by Greek philosophers, Roman naturalists, Arabian doctors and medieval monks. It is no wonder that botanists speak a strange language. The rivalry between Eve and Linnaeus ought to be friendly, for their names are used for different purposes by different people, but it is not altogether so; 'I who cannot tolerate English names in any shape', Hooker writes to Asa Gray. Even the gardener's boy speaks of a Dianthus, despising the names Carnation, Pink and Picotee. Perhaps Antirrhinum, False Nose, suits his youthful mind, but he has outgrown so childish a name as Snapdragon. Some people, on the other hand, consider the botanical names barbarous, though they are classical in their orderliness and mostly in their origin. We should not be prejudiced, though Eve is our mother and Linnaeus did not greatly like the English.

Botanists have not followed Eve's example, or at least Adam's, in assigning to every creature a name peculiar to its nature; they have assigned too many of their own names. Linnaeus himself is called after a famous Lime tree that grew in his neighbourhood – Lime, also the name of a more fruitful tree, was Line or Lynd, as in Lyndhurst – and a plant is named after him, the pretty Linnaea of northern woods; L'Obel, a Flemish botanist who lived in England, takes his name from some Abele or White Poplar, and he has given it to the Lobelias, one of which is common in our tarns; usually, however, there is not this give and take. If Linnaeus only consented to the name Linnaea, he encouraged the practice of calling plants after botanists; Bartsia, a melancholy plant of summer fields, he called after his friend, Dr Bartsch. No one will complain that Virgil, whom John Martyn considered not only a poet but an accomplished botanist, has given his name to a plant, or Goethe, who expounded the famous botanical theory of metamorphosis, or even Crabbe, almost the only English poet to take an interest in botany; nor will anyone complain that the many-sided Ray has given his name to a plant as well as to a fish; but it may be thought that the practice has conferred on some botanists a cheap immortality. Linnaeus himself was well aware of the immortality he conferred; recalling how Augustus Caesar raised a statue to Antonius Musa for curing him with Lettuces, and Juba, King of Mauretania, caused a plant to be called Euphorbia after Euphorbus, his own doctor and Antonius Musa's brother, Linnaeus cries:

Where now is Musa's statue? It has perished, it has disappeared! But the memorial of Euphorbus endures perennially and can never be thrown down.

Here then is the explanation of many familiar names. Gardenia, a proud relation of the Bedstraws, is so named, not because it grows in gardens, but after an American botanist, Dr Garden. Buddleia, coming from China, might be thought to be named after Buddha, but it is after a country clergyman, Adam Buddle. Magnolia, a grand-sounding name for a grandiose plant, is named only after a Frenchman, Magnol. That we mispronounce Dahlia is clear from its derivation from a Dr Dahl. Wild plants, too, though mostly rare ones, are so named, such as Galinsoga,

Achillea, siue Millefolium nobile.
Achilles Yarrow.

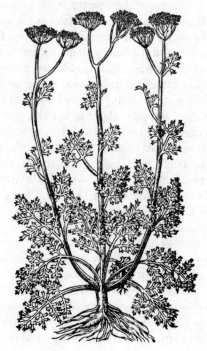

Sibbaldia and Thale Cress. I long imagined Teesdalia was named after a favourite haunt of botanists, but it is named after a gardener at Castle Howard. Are these the plants of which Tennyson speaks,

Flowers of all heavens and lovelier than their names?[3]

Contrasted with the practice of making a tombstone of a plant is the practice of making a joke. Was Dioscorides serious when he named a very spiny tree Acacia, Good Nature? Was Pliny right in saying that the Arbutus or Strawberry tree was called Unedo, I Eat One, because no one would want to eat two of its fruits? Ovid puts it among the fruits with which the one-eyed Polyphemus tried to tempt Galatea. Why is Bearberry, with its small bitter berries, called Arctostaphylos Uva-Ursi, which is first Greek and then Latin for Bear's Grapes? On the other hand Sainfoin, Wholesome Hay, has the botanical name Onobrychis, Making an Ass Bray, no doubt at the sight of such rich fodder. Have the gods changed their habits since Homer's time, or is there a joke in the name of the plant that gives us cocoa, Theobroma, Food of the Gods? If the mother of Euripides could make a living by selling Watercress, how did it come to have the name Nasturtium, Nose-twister?

But what are we to think of the botanical names themselves, that is, apart from their value for botanists? Achillea Millefolium (Yarrow) has an Homeric sound. It is a combination of the plant's two old names; the botanists called it Achillea, supposing it the herb with which Achilles healed his Myrmidons, while apothecaries gave it the more popular name, Millefolium, Plant with a Thousand Leaves. Scrophularia (Figwort), on the other hand, is not an attractive name; let us hope the plant was a better cure for scrofula, or the king's evil, than Queen Anne's hand on young Samuel Johnson. And the name's leprosy has infected the other members of its large family, so that Speedwell, Foxglove, Mullein and Snapdragon are classed as Scrophulari-aceae. Rousseau thought highly of the botanical names; in his *Letters to a Young Lady* he advises her to learn them, for they are, he says,

3. 'The Princess'.

all Latin or Greek, expressive, short, sonorous, and even form elegant constructions by their extreme precision.

Southey expresses a different opinion in *The Doctor*:

> As for the scientific names of Plants, – if Apollo had not lost all power he would have elongated the ears of Tournefort and Linnaeus, and all their followers, as deservedly as he did those of Midas.

That it is well to learn them I know from experience. Meeting a South Kensington botanist in Edinburgh, I asked about a rare Saxifrage, careful to give the botanical name so that there should be no mistake. He told me it grew on the Pentland Hills, even describing the spot. That seemed incredible, but who was I to set myself against South Kensington? The way led by a talkative burn and, still unbelieving, I took it into my confidence, 'Tell me, little burn, is there a rare Alpine plant growing on your bank?' but though

With an inner voice the river ran,[4]

I could not interpret its reply. I came in sight of a lonely cottage, the kind of cottage I have learnt to suspect, for if it happens to be a gamekeeper's, the pursuit of botany may change to the pursuit of the botanist. When gamekeepers shout from a distance I am liable to fits of deafness; this time a gamekeeper straddled my path like Apollyon confronting Christian, and with the same command, to turn and go back. I sat down and began to eat my lunch. I ate it very slowly, stopping to tempt a shy meadow-pipit with crumbs, a humanitarian action that seemed to annoy the gamekeeper. At last I rose and turned away, but as soon as I was hidden by a bend of the steep bank, I struck off, and making a wide detour, rejoined the burn beyond the cottage. 'Is it worth it?' I asked, for I remembered what a Scottish botanist had said about the plant, 'high up the mountain in cold eastern corries'. My faith was at a low ebb, when I suddenly recognized the spot that had been described. I hurried forward, and the sight of the common Yellow Mountain Saxifrage raised my hope for the rarer plant. But it was not there, and I wandered about sadly, thinking hard things of South Kensington botanists. Then, my eye lighting on one of the yellow flowers, I stopped short; a

4. Tennyson: 'The Dying Swan'.

thought flashed through my mind – could it be? – yes, there is no doubt – such a botanist would not make a mistake – he had indeed directed me to the spot. There grew the plant I had asked for; unfortunately, confusing the botanical names, I had asked for Yellow Mountain Saxifrage.

That incident taught me the important lesson, that I should learn the botanical names; but, strangely enough, it also taught me just the opposite lesson, that I should leave them alone. 'Learn them', said Linnaeus; 'Don't trouble', said my mother Eve. My indulgent mother has spoilt me, for it is the second lesson I have learnt. Yet more than once I had paid for my ignorance. One day a local botanist said, 'I suppose you know Campanula rotundi-folia'. Round-leaved Bell-flower, I thought; I know Nettle-leaved and Ivy-leaved, but Round-leaved is something new. So he took me for a long walk to see this rarity, and when we came to the place, 'There,' he said, and I said 'Where?' 'There,' he insisted, and to my astonishment pointed to a Scotch Bluebell. So that was what I had come to see? But how was I to know it was rare in some parts of the country? Or how imagine a plant with leaves so hairlike that it is sometimes called Hairbell should be described as round-leaved? Later I learnt that as a seedling it has round leaves; but few people notice this plant till its flowers appear as from nowhere, like stars in the evening sky.

The chief disadvantage of Eve's names is that, like ourselves, they suffer from Mutabilitie. Horace might have been thinking of them when he said,

At each year's fall the forests change their leaves; even so the old race of words passes away.

Some names have fluttered about like insects, trying here and there, before they came to rest on a flower. Forget-me-not was given to Ground Pine before

> The mouse-ear looked with bright blue eyes,
> And said 'Forget-me-not'.

Gillyflower flirted with several flowers; now it has flown away, leaving behind it Stock, which is only half a name. A Stock is a Gillyflower that grows on a stocky stem as contrasted with another Gillyflower, the Pink, that grows on a spindly one. But

Stocks were also called Violets, so that an upright plant of the ditches, which ought to be called Water-primrose, was called Water-violet, because it looked like a Stock. Botanical names on the other hand are almost all fixed, like the insect's effigy in a Bee Orchid. And Eve's names vary, not only from time to time, but even more from place to place; the tree in England called Sycamore is called in Scotland Plane – it is thought to have Plane-like leaves. Often it is hard to say what plant is intended by a name, as in Clare's poem, 'Insects':

> Then, to the heath-bell's silken hood they fly,
> And like to princes in their slumbers lie,
> Secure from night, and dropping dews, and all,
> In silken beds and roomy painted hall.

Usually Heath-bell is the same as Heather-bell, but the Harebell is more likely to provide flies with a roomy night's lodging, and perhaps a small supper of honey or pollen as well. Yet in spite of all the disadvantages of Eve's names we will not sigh with Mrs Browning

> For a poet's tongue of baptismal flame
> To call the tree or the flower by its name![5]

We could not trust even a poet; Dryden refused in his version of the Aeneid to translate Amaracus by Sweet Marjoram:

If I shou'd translate it Sweet-Marjoram, as the Word signifies; the Reader wou'd think I had mistaken *Virgil*: For those Village-words, as I may call them, give us a mean Idea of the thing.

Eve may be said to have done her work well enough. Some of her names are vulgar, though their vulgarity is not always apparent; but these we may safely attribute to Adam. (Yet was Eve so refined that she would have approved of Bridges calling St John's-wort Sinjunwort? As the plant is named after the Baptist, about whose feast-day it flowers, he has not the authority of the curate who spoke of the Gospel according to Sinjun.) Plants that cured ailments, such as Squinancy-wort, a cure for quinsy, and Scabious for the scab, are not pleasantly named; but, like rolling stones that do gather moss, such current words take

5. 'The North and the South'.

on associations that hide the original meaning. It would be a loss, however, not to recognize in Centaury one of the plants with which the centaur Chiron taught the youthful Achilles medicine, and I confess that no name affects me so much as Woundwort, which makes me see a soldier, escaped from a battle in the Wars of the Roses, laying leaves on his wounds. We must admit that some of Eve's names are incorrect; neither Bulrush nor Flowering Rush is really a Rush; but how could we expect Eve, 'poor motherless Eve', to show a knowledge of family relationships? On the other hand many of Eve's names are almost worthy of the plants, such as Restharrow, given to a plant whose stubborn roots can arrest a harrow. Some look mysterious; we might wonder at the three names given to a northern umbellifer, Spignel, Meu and Baldmoney. No doubt the familiar names will seem the best, for these, in spite of what Juliet says of the Rose and its name, cannot be disentangled from the flowers themselves. But there is one name in which, quite apart from the plant, the crawling Bramble whose autumn-bronzed leaves are beautiful on the mountains, Eve, as I think, reaches perfection: the name, Cloudberry. A woman who lived at the foot of the Moorfoot Hills used to say, 'You must come and taste my Cloudberry jam'; how thankful I am that I never went; I might have thought less of the name. As it is, I feel that compared with that one beautiful name, Cloudberry, all the botanical names are 'not worth a leke'.

If that judgment seems intemperate, it must be partly put down to a glass of rum. One day in a Cornish town I went into a chemist's shop, but the chemist shook his head and advised me to go to the Wesleyan minister. I was not dying myself, nor concerned about a dying friend; I merely wanted information about a plant. When I entered the minister's study I was cheered by the sight of botanical journals I should not have cared to read, and the minister himself welcomed me with a Wesleyan warmth. But when I asked if he knew where Bladderseed grew, a look of pain crossed his face, as though I had reminded him of an internal complaint. But no, he sprang up from his chair and began to discourse on the need for botanical names. 'I correspond with botanists on the Continent,' he said; 'they understand me, and I understand them, for we speak the same language.' At first I looked up with timid interest, but having heard it all before I took the opportunity, as he went on, to consult a book I drew from my pocket; then, when he finished, I said, 'I mean Physospermum cornubiense.' 'Ah, that's better,' he cried, though in fact I thought he was somewhat taken aback. He appeared to consider for a few minutes and then asked if I had a map. 'You will find it there,' he said, pointing with his pencil. 'It's a long way from here,' I said doubtfully. 'But that's the spot,' he replied.

Some hours later motorists, racing along the main road, must have wondered at a rain-drenched figure wandering about a lonely part of Bodmin Moor. But I did not wander long; for when a wise old botanist of Launceston, named Wise, later asked me laughingly, 'Did you really expect to find it there?' I replied, 'I did and I didn't'. I was soon plodding along the road, getting wetter and wetter, but thankful I was making for a place marked on the map Jamaica Inn. At first I thought of a glass of beer, but I began to entertain more ambitious ideas, and 'Why not a glass of rum?' I asked. Such an idea would not have occurred to me but for the name, Jamaica Inn; but as it had occurred, I felt in my wet and shivery condition it was only wisdom. That the Wesleyan minister would not approve made me smile; had he not driven me to it, sending me on a fool's errand rather than admit he knew nothing of the plant? I even saw in that glass of rum a kind of revenge. But when I entered the inn and pleasantly made my demand, an impudent girl told me I was in a temperance hotel. So in the end I was doubly deceived, by the discourse on botanical names and by the name, Jamaica Inn. Is it any wonder I felt a bitterness towards them both? It might, however, have been drowned in that glass of rum.

20 Types of Botanist

While many botanists have described the various types of plants, no one so far as I know has described the various types of botanist. Theophrastus, both as author of the famous *Characters* and as lecturer in botany under Aristotle, could best have undertaken the task. All I offer is a few illustrations, and even these in no way concern the botanist proper, the man of science, but only the kind of botanist who might be called Botanicus Pseudo-botanicus. Nothing derogatory of course is implied in the name; is not the beautiful Wild Daffodil called Narcissus Pseudo-narcissus?

An account of plants usually begins with the Buttercup family, which offers in the common Buttercup a simple type of plant; so I begin with our Village Schoolmistress, who is certainly a simple type of botanist. She invites the children to bring wild flowers to school, and she seldom fails to give them a name. Botanists are divided into two classes, 'splitters' and 'lumpers', 'splitters' being those who split plants into a large number of species and subspecies, while 'lumpers', impatient of minute distinctions, are inclined to lump them together. Our Village Schoolmistress carries lumping to an extreme degree; most spring flowers, that are white or lilac, she lumps together as Milkmaids. But one day she was puzzled; a child brought her a plant with large white flowers such as no one in our village had seen before. As this was in summer, clearly it could not be accommodated by the convenient name, Milkmaid; but so far from being damaged, her reputation was enhanced when she said she would send it to Kew. The children eagerly waited Kew's answer. For days it did not come, as though Kew were hard at work on the problem, perhaps indeed finding it too difficult; but when at last it did come, it was – White Foxglove. 'Was it really just a White

Foxglove?' I asked her afterwards with mock seriousness. 'Yes, I think there was no doubt about it', she replied.

A better botanist I call the Fair Widow, though I could not decide whether her hair was fair or turning grey. Staying in a Cornish town and learning that she was the local authority on plants, I paid her a visit. When I inquired about Cornish Moneywort (a trailing plant often grown in greenhouses), she offered to show it to me herself. Seldom have I had a more embarrassing experience than I had with the Fair Widow. When we passed on the way the pretty little Ivy-leaved Bellflower, she invited me to bend down and listen to its fairy chimes. She asked if I had studied the legends of flowers, and when I emphatically said 'No', she misunderstood the emphasis, taking it to mean I was anxious to learn. So we had to stand in the road while she told me stories which, if she had not described one as a beautiful Persian legend and another as a delightful old German tale, I should have thought the silliest stories I had ever heard. When we came on a Common Cudweed, the Herba impia of old botanists, she asked if I knew why it was called the Impious Herb. I hastily answered 'Yes', but that did not save me from hearing, for she stopped a passing countryman and, pointing to the plant, asked him the same question. When he shook his head, she explained it was because the shoots had overtopped the stem, like children disrespectful of their parents. The man stared at it in a puzzled way, and still shaking his head moved on without a word. I feared I was a disappointment to the Fair Widow, but I was wrong. When we returned from seeing Cornish Moneywort, she said, 'There is something I should like to show you'. She led me into a Wesleyan chapel, and we stood before a marble tablet on the wall; it was a memorial to her husband drowned at sea. As we turned away from it she said quietly, 'I knew you would understand'. So I had made a friend after all.

Though the Colonel was a much more advanced botanist than the Fair Widow, I never understood why he took an interest in plants, unless it was that he had a fast sports-car and a wife who liked her lunch out-of-doors. He sped about the country, bringing back news of some rare plant he had discovered, and the climax came when he announced that he had found Summer

Lady's-tresses in the New Forest. I heard of it through a common friend, who told me the story. The Colonel chanced to enter a shop, and there on the counter he saw a glass with some flowers. He stared at them, and stared harder, and then 'What have you here?' he asked the shopman. 'Autumn Lady's-tresses', replied the shopman. 'No, they are Summer Lady's-tresses; and Good Heavens!' thundered the Colonel, 'you have picked a dozen plants'. The shopman was dumbfounded. 'Where did you find them?' demanded the Colonel. The shopman told him where, a bog a few miles away. Sternly warning him never to pick another plant and not to breathe a word about it to anyone, the Colonel sprang into his car and dashed off to find the plant for himself. Having heard this, I called on the Colonel; he confirmed the story, and said 'I frightened the fellow out of his wits'. 'Extraordinary', I remarked, adding casually, 'and where was the bog?' But the Colonel was too sharp; shaking his head, 'I am afraid I could not describe the place', he replied. Fortunately he had mentioned the name of the town and the nature of the shop; so a few days later I presented myself before the shopman. I have always believed that few people can keep a secret, and my faith in this shopman was not misplaced. At first he was unwilling to speak, but I explained I was a friend of the Colonel; how else could I have heard of the plant? So he directed me to the bog, but it took me so long to find it, that I had no time to look for the plant, a greenish Orchid difficult to detect. The following summer I was back in the bog, and though I made a careful search, again I failed. Fearing the shopman had played me false, I interviewed him on my way to the station; he assured me my mistake was in coming a fortnight too soon. These journeys to the New Forest were long and difficult; not possessing a sports-car, I had to travel by a series of cheap day tickets on the railway, jumping off at stations and hastily buying a ticket for the next stage. The third summer, however, I tried again and found the plant. Feeling I had scored off the Colonel, I said to him one day in the street, 'You once gave yourself away'. 'How?' he asked sharply, and I told him my story. But it was now 'caviare to the colonel'; he was not even interested; as I heard afterwards, he had given up botany and was devoting himself to bridge.

The Old Man was not as good a botanist as the Colonel, but

even in his old age he was keen to see or hear some new thing. I had again made the now familiar journey to the New Forest. Dropping in on the same shopman I was greeted with 'What are you after this time?' 'Isnardia', I said, and his eyes opened. 'Could you take my old father with you?' he asked eagerly. 'It's rather a long way', I pointed out. 'Oh, he won't mind', he replied. So I called at the house where the Old Man lived with his son, and 'I'll come', he said promptly. He was so old that he could hardly walk, but he hobbled along the road with great determination. When I saved his life several times by pulling him out of the way of a passing car, he seemed to resent it. As he kept mopping his face, I suggested we might sit down and rest, but 'If you want to rest, I'll wait for you', he replied. At last I led him into an open glade and said, 'Somewhere here'. 'Have you brought a description of it?' he asked. 'No', I replied. He stopped and stared at me with 'Then how will you know it?' 'I shall know it when I see something I don't know', I answered with an airy assurance. 'Yours is a queer way of botanizing', he remarked. Perhaps he was right; when I had spent the best part of an hour wandering about without any idea of what I was looking for, I began to think it was not the best of all possible ways. 'Are you sure this is the place?' he kept calling; 'Quite sure', I shouted back with a confidence I was far from feeling. That our search was useless we both seemed to realize when we met and flung overselves down on a grassy mound. I waited for him to speak, and was even prepared with my reply. 'Well, I never asked you to come.' I think he was just about to speak, when I sprang up crying, 'We are sitting on it'. 'Sitting on what?' he asked, looking quickly around. 'The barrow', I shouted. 'What barrow? What are you talking about?' he cried; but I was already running down to a ditch that separated the glade from the surrounding trees. Words I had heard from an old Southampton botanist years before had suddenly come back, 'a ditch opposite a grassy mound that looks like a prehistoric barrow'. I had noticed a mean-looking plant in the ditch, but had dismissed it as some kind of Water-purslane. Now I bent over it and 'Is this Isnardia?' I called. The Old Man hurried down, almost falling over himself; he looked at it for a moment or two, and then said 'No'. The hope that had flickered went out. As it seemed hopeless to renew the search, we started to walk back. I had observed that he put a specimen of the plant in his vasculum; now I observed that several times he opened the vasculum and peeped in, without, however, making any remark. I grew suspicious; could it be Isnardia after all? I might have asked, but I felt he would not welcome the question; he appeared to be intent only on getting home. As we approached the town, his hobbling pace quickened, and when we reached the street where he lived, he was almost running. At the gate I expected to be invited into the house, but no, he left me standing outside. In a few minutes he appeared with a book under his arm, which I recognized as *Hayward's Botanist's Pocket-book*. 'Come along', he said, as though for some reason the book could not be opened in that street. He is going to his son's shop, I thought, but I was wrong; he pushed open a glass door marked Public Bar. As I meekly followed, I knew the plant in the ditch was Isnardia. The Old Man had slyly consulted his Hayward in the house; all that remained was a formal identification, with means at hand to celebrate the occasion.

The botanist I knew best – he directed me to many plants – I call the Missionary. Looking through a catalogue of second-hand books on religion, I once came on a curious item, *Seventy Years Among Savages*, by Henry S. Salt. The title suggested that the author, like St Teresa, had aspired to become a martyr at a tender age, but living so long, had singularly failed. But the book had been wrongly catalogued under Religion; the author's mission was to meat-eating savages in this country. I could imagine a clergyman, surprised he had not heard of this devoted missionary, buying the book, and discovering to his indignation that he himself was one of the savages Henry S. Salt laboured so many years to convert. Certainly he would demand his money back. Yet I like to think of the writer as a Missionary.

The chief reason why he regarded Englishmen as savages was, not that they killed and ate one another, a practice he might have commended, but that they killed and ate animals; for Salt was a vegetarian. Naturally he was sarcastic about hunting:

> I could not love thee, Deer, so much
> Loved I not hunting more;

and he would have agreed with Byron that Isaac Walton,

> The quaint, old cruel coxcomb, in his gullet
> Should have a hook, and a small trout to pull it.[1]

But come to think of it, why did he stand up for the rights of animals, and not for the rights of plants? Is it not wrong to kill and eat a Cabbage? Or nibble a nut, which, unless it happens to be a dead one, lives and breathes like ourselves? Ought we not to keep to fruits, escaping the curse pronounced on Adam after his fall, 'Thou shalt eat the herb of the field'? These problems arise from the fact that we are less civilized than plants, or, to speak more exactly, less advanced in Practical Chemistry. Green plants manufacture food from the beggarly elements of air and water, but our chemists can manufacture it to only a negligible extent. So, directly, or indirectly through animals, we prey on plants. We are worse savages than Salt thought.

Nay further [says Sir Thomas Browne], we are what we all abhor, *Anthropophagi* and Cannibals, devourers not only of men, but of our selves; for all this mass of flesh which we behold, came in at our mouths; this frame we look upon, hath been upon our trenchers; in brief, we have devour'd our selves.[2]

It is no wonder that Plotinus was so much ashamed of his body that he refused to tell Porphyry when his birthday was, and Cleombrotus, after reading the Phaedo, flung himself into the sea. Salt of course, as a vegetarian, was the worst of savages, for after all, who are we that we should eat plants? Ought we not seriously to reconsider what Swift called *A Modest Proposal for Eating Irish Children*? Some simple-minded person may say, 'But surely a human being is of more consideration than a plant?' Landor at least did not think so, for when, having flung his cook out of the window and realizing what he had done, he rushed to look down on the garden, where no doubt the man lay writhing with a broken limb, conscience-smitten he exclaimed, 'Good God, I forgot the violets'.

1. *Don Juan.*
2. *Religio Medici.*

21 Sketches

Travelling one day in a bus from Falmouth to Truro, a journey new to me, I was looking idly at the landscape, a broad valley curiously cut by pits and water-courses, when I suddenly sat up and said, 'I have been here before'. I had heard of people who, visiting a place for the first time, had an unaccountable sense of familiarity with it; a friend had even told me he had burst into reminiscent tears among

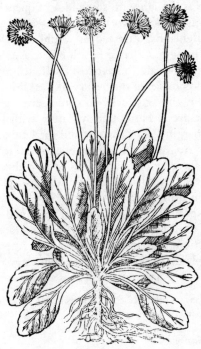

Bellis media sylueſtris.
The middle wilde Daiſie.

the ruins of Babylon; now I was thrilled to think such an experience had come my way. For there was no doubt about it; the valley was too peculiar to be confused with any valley I had seen elsewhere. I unfolded a map and was tracing my journey, when I noticed two things, a pencil-dot and in the margin the faded letters C.H. 'Oh!' I said, and sat back and reflected.

While most of our plants, especially the common ones such as Daisy and Dandelion, came from Central Europe after the Ice Age, travelling by land over what is now the North Sea, a number of others, found chiefly in Cornwall and Devon and also in Ireland, appear to have come from the south-west corner of Europe. Some botanists, to explain their presence, conjure from the sea the lost land of Lyonesse; others, commenting on the smallness of the seeds, point to the wind and birds as a likely means of transport. While Cornish Heath, the best known of them, keeps more or less to the Lizard, a few have wandered far afield, Burning Lobelia to the New Forest, stopping at the Cat and Fiddle Inn as though with some idea of quenching its thirst: Pale or Portuguese Butterwort, an insect-eating plant, even to the Western Highlands, attracted, it would seem, by favourable reports of the midges. Ciliated Heath has strayed to one or two places, but might be said to have lost itself; at least it is difficult to find. As it is considered the beauty of the Heath family, I was anxious to see it and was lucky to come across a botanist who knew where it grew. He dotted my map with his pencil and wrote in the margin C.H. The dot and the letters now brought back the misty August day I had set out to find it in this valley. So I had been there before! What I failed to realize was that this place I had reached by bus from Falmouth was a place I had once reached by train from Truro.

But if my experience was not after all abnormal, it was at least unusual, for of most places where I have found a rare flower I keep a clear recollection. Perhaps I attach as much importance to the place as to the plant. To search for rare plants might seem a super-fluity of naughtiness, if the common ones are as good or better.

I saw clearly [says Traherne] that there is a real valuableness in all the common things: in the scarce a feigned.[1]

1. *Centuries of Meditations.*

But I have sometimes felt that my search was inspired by more than the plants themselves, perhaps by the confused idea that such plants, being so rare, are not quite of this world and might take me a little out of it. One might imagine them those plants seen by Dante in the Earthly Paradise, sometimes mysteriously wafted to this world by the wind. Also there is this to be said: having found a rare plant I carry away a picture of the place. Naaman the leper took back to Syria two mules' burden of the soil of Canaan, but I have carried away a mountain or a bog or a rocky shore. The place remains in my memory along with the plant, being indeed a kind of Elysian Fields,

> Where falls not hail, or rain, or any snow,
> Nor ever wind blows loudly.[2]

But let us hope the plant propagated itself on earth, for in my memory it will find but a temporary immortality.

So of plants and places I have made a kind of *Liber Studiorum*, charming sketches, I who cannot draw a line. Common plants are there as well, not of course as plants seen in any particular place,

> But those that *Plato* saw, *Ideas* nam'd,
> Daughters of Jove, for heavenly Extract fam'd;
> Etherial plants![3]

They grow, not by themselves, but in flowery societies. Talking to a stranger once in a train I said, 'So you are a botanist'; to which he replied, 'I am an ecologist'. For a moment I was astonished, imagining an ecologist must be a writer of eclogues; but I soon discovered it meant a student of plants as they grow in local communities. Ecologists study plants, not individually, but in groups, each group being itself an entity. They say to one another what Gwydion said to Math:

'Come now and let us make a wife for Llew'.

Of these two, Gwydion and Math, Francis Ledwidge says:

> They took the violet and the meadow-sweet
> To form her pretty face, and for her feet

2. Tennyson: 'The Passing of Arthur'.
3. *Liber Plantarum*.

> They built a mound of daisies on a wing,
> And for her voice they made a linnet sing
> In the wide poppy blowing for her mouth.[4]

Ecologists, however, do not mix up plants in that way, but take them as they grow in one or another set of natural conditions. Such a group is the opposite of a garden; in fact, if an ecologist caught sight of a garden, he would probably scream and run away. So it is that plants grow together in my sketches. I exercise of course a certain artistic licence, omitting the various Grasses, Rushes and what-nots, of which I do not know the names.

Perhaps it is the sketch of a slow stream. Most water-plants are thought to have been land-plants once, having been driven by competition to seek refuge by the water, like the lake-dwellers at Meare in the Early Iron Age. One can imagine them still in various stages of retreat. Iris, usually identified with the chivalrous Fleur-de-lys, 'a sword for its leaf, and a lily for its heart', fights a rearward action by the bank. In the water itself Reedmace waves its heavy weapon, and Arrowhead, sometimes called Water Archer, points its Parthian darts. Skullcap, though protected by a blue helmet, is half over the bank, while Amphibious Persicaria, afraid to stay on land or take to the water, crawls in a muddy bay. Frogbit, as befits its timid name, floats rootlessly on the stream. Like Water Plantain it has only three petals; perhaps it dropped one when it fled. Who knows what Duckweed may have lost on the way? A relation of the lordly Palm, it now only forms a scum,

> the green mantle of the standing pool.[5]

Hornwort, a strange plant with no known relations, has plunged under the water; it grows entirely

> Where harmlesse fish monastique silence keepe,[6]

waving its mossy head as though in wonder how it lives by being drowned.

Or it my be the sketch of a chalk-hill. Wind blows cloud-shadows across the Grass that vainly tries to uproot itself and

4. 'The Wife of Llew'.
5. *King Lear*.
6. Donne: 'Elegie on Mrs Boulstred'.

follow. It disturbs the Nodding Thistle in its sleep, but not the Dwarf Thistle that lies too close to the ground, so close that it looks like a beheaded flower. It ruffles Salad Burnet, feeding its invisible body on the cucumber scent, but flees from the mousy smell of Hound's-tongue. Aromatic plants have their perfumes blown about and confused, so that Thyme smells of Marjoram and Basil of Calamint. Cinnabar Moths rock on the Rampion, a strangely beautiful flower like a blue sea-anemone, deserving its unique botanical name, Phyteuma, the Plant. The Rock-rose's petals quiver, as though their gold were melting in the sun; even Yellow-wort, a Gentian that appears too prim to admit those marriage-brokers, the bees, bends from its waxen stiffness in the general excitement of the hill.

Such sketches of stream and hill, made at no particular time or place, are not real; they fade like the vision of Poor Susan at the Corner of Wood Street:

> The stream will not flow, and the hill will not rise.[7]

Sketches made on the spot are better, such as 'A Distant View of Salisbury Cathedral with Pheasant's-eye in the Foreground'. Yet even in that sketch

> Dry seas, with golden surges, ebb and flow,[8]

half-hiding the cornfield flower, our only scarlet flower apart from Pimpernel and Poppy. So too in 'Candytuft on the Chiltern Hills' the small white flower is scarcely noticeable; I have to enliven the sketch by introducing Blue Cornflower and Corn Cockle. I choose these for their colour, and also because with the purification of the farmer's seed they are becoming scarce; they have not Charlock's craft to drop the seeds before the corn is cut. (Why should I not introduce a few plants in a sketch? Botticelli has more than thirty in his picture, *Spring*.) In 'Golden Samphire on the Cornish Coast' the flower shows to better effect. Here the seas are not dry:

> Their billows break their hearts against the shore,[9]

7. Wordsworth.
8. Benlowes: 'The Pleasures of Retirement'.
9. Patrick Hannay: 'The Second Elegy'.

splashing the flower. Samphire, a corruption of St Pierre, means the plant that grows on a rock. Two plants claim the distinction of being named after St Peter, just as at one time there were two rival Popes. Golden Samphire is much the rarer, so perhaps it is the other, Sea Samphire – we might call it Shakespeare's Samphire – that has the better title to catholicity.

How differently the waves break in 'A Jersey Bay'! They fall slowly over with a thud, spreading a broad net of foam on the sand. Perhaps they are tired in the heat, for while I have known the sun so hot on a Scottish mountain-top that I was glad to bathe my hands in the shadow of a stone, it was even fiercer that August afternoon I made the sketch. How surprising then to see in the shingle a plant so downy that it appears to be wrapt in cotton-wool, called in fact Cottonweed! I have long held the theory that our best protection against a warm summer sun is a thick woollen overcoat. I feel no need to test the theory when so many downy plants grow in hot arid places, such as Great Sea-stock, growing in this same bay, and of course Mullein, sometimes called Flannel Flower. Their down keeps in the moisture and keeps out the heat. I admit, however, that some mountain plants, such as Dwarf Cudweed, are downy for the reverse reason, to keep in the heat and keep out the moisture; so perhaps it is permissible to wear a thick overcoat in winter as well.

My strangest sketch is called 'Cronkley Fells'. Though it was made on a bridge in Teesdale, it might as well have been in a fog in London, that 'City of Dreadful Nocturnes'. The mistiness of Carrière's pictures is far outdone, for in this sketch there is nothing to be seen. The flower itself, Twisted-podded Whitlow-grass, is hidden behind more than a mile of mist; so thick was the mist that day

That all things one, and one as nothing was.[10]

I made the sketch when I came down from the fells, looking back with thankfulness that I had come down at all, and still more that I had struck the bridge. 'The Devil's Kitchen, North Wales' is a much finer sketch. It shows two of the rarest plants growing together, Snow Saxifrage and Spiderwort. They appear

10. *Faerie Queene.*

on the walls of that dangerous chasm through which, a thousand feet below, gleams Llyn Idwal. Any Welshman – if he could see it – would pronounce this sketch sublime. I think so myself; in fact I feel inclined to say with Nero, 'What an artist perishes in me!' If only I could draw!

'Diana, or The Tables Turned' can hardly be called a sketch; it is more like a dream, for in the manner of a dream the scene changes, though only from a bog to a brook. What plants grow in that New Forest Bog is not clear; perhaps Buckbean, a Gentian that disgraces its prim relations by growing in such a place, Bog Pimpernel, trailing about like a long green millipede with pink bells, Marsh St John's-wort, its small flowers glittering like sly gold nuggets from the grey leaves; indeed I scarcely looked to see, as I floundered in the bog, my mind divided between the hope of finding Bog Orchid and the fear of being swallowed up like Korah, Dathan and Abiram. Bog Orchid is a small greenish plant that one might be staring at and yet not see; though I knew it was there, it was so difficult to detect that the bog was becoming a Slough of Despond. At last I found it and waded to the bank. Viewing myself I said in the words of the Scottish poet,

Ay, fegs, an' fat dae ye think o' my legs?[11]

But the remedy for my African legs was at hand, and here the scene changes to a neighbouring brook. I undressed and lay back in the water, anchored by my elbows. I trusted the trees would shade me from encroaching eyes, but I reckoned without Diana. No one knows how huge an animal a horse is till he has seen one leaping over his naked body. The horse mistook me for a water-god, for it reared violently on the bank; Diana looked round to see if I was a drowned corpse. She was soon satisfied and disappeared through the trees. Other hunters leapt the brook farther down. Two men approached, but finding nothing to say, turned and rode on; I suppose they were after a fox, not an otter. I lay in the brook and thought how Actaeon, having seen Diana bathe, was changed to a stag and fled from his own hounds; this time the tables were turned, for it was Diana who fled.

I never thought I should make a film, but what else can I call

11. Charles Murray.

'Wicken Fen'? It starts in Cambridge, in the house of a friend, whom I am earnestly advising to visit Wicken Fen; 'the last piece of original fenland in England', I tell him: 'the home of the Swallow-tail Butterfly'. 'Is it some wild flower you want to see?' he asks impatiently; 'Two', I reply, and the matter is settled. Later in the day we are seen setting off in his car. I sit back and enjoy the expanse of flat landscape, where

The trenchèd waters run from sky to sky;[12]

but suddenly I look anxious. A flash-back in the film explains this. I appear again in Cambridge, several hours earlier, wondering whether I should apply for a permit. Anyone can see I smile at the idea; who can prevent my walking on to a fen? Besides, such a thing would be against my principles. But now – for I have resumed my interrupted journey – I view with concern the deep dykes not to be crossed except by a bridge. When three towers rise in the distance, small yet somehow grand, I almost suggest to my friend I should prefer to visit Ely Cathedral. As we approach the entrance to the fen I am struck with consternation; a man, no doubt the keeper, stands in the middle of the road with outstretched arms. As we step out of the car, 'Welcome, gentlemen; you have come to see the Swallow-tail Butterfly', he cries, and lurches forward as though to embrace us. Supposing his chief business is to protect that precious creature, I hastily explain we are botanists who would like to see Milk Parsley and Blue March Vetchling. 'Come along', he replies, and leads the way across a bridge. I mark his unsteady gait, which I associate with his effusive welcome and forgetfulness of the permit. But what is happening to myself? I too feel unsteady on that spongy fen. And here the film takes an astonishing turn; I am suddenly changed to a primitive man, flung back, not a few hours, but thousands of years, back to the beginning of things. Not only Wicken Fen, the whole earth is shaking under my feet. Cambridge no longer exists, because it never has existed. Nothing is real; all knowledge vanishes away; I am down on bedrock, this shaking earth.

My most beautiful sketch was made on Canisp, a mountain in Sutherland. The mist was so thick at first that only the cairn told

12. Tennyson: 'Ode to Memory'.

me I stood on the top of a mountain; even the cairn, when I stepped a few yards away, disappeared in remote distance. A small yellow flower growing in the rocks caught my eye. I recognized it as a kind of Golden-rod, but what kind I did not know. A specimen I picked I sent next day to a botanist. His son wrote some weeks later, saying that his father, before he died, had been greatly interested in the plant; he thought it might be Solidago cambrica, but was not sure it was not a new species; meanwhile the specimen had been lost. Perhaps it was that Solidago, an Alpine Golden-rod, but it might have been some plant that no botanist has seen or will see. Common Golden-rod, held in the hand, is said to reveal hidden treasure; but as I held this small Golden-rod in my hand, the mist began to part, showing me something more wonderful, the earth as I had never seen it before. What I saw was a multitude of hummocks and shining lochans, yet all so strange and beautiful that in looking down on the earth I might have been looking up to heaven. It was the rarest of those rare occasions, which I have known only in the Western Highlands, when earth becomes its own artist, revealing itself with an unearthly beauty, so that I have said, 'One day in thy courts is better than a thousand'. To say the earth is its own artist is hardly a figure of speech, for I felt it was showing me something I could not have seen for myself. So my sketch from Canisp is only a copy; when I think of the original I say, 'Earth, I shall never see you so beautiful again, never again

> Clamber the azure mountaines, thrown so high,
> And fetch from thence thy faire Idea just,
> That in those sunny courts doth hidden lie,
> Cloath'd with such light, as blinds the Angels eye'. [13]

---

13. Giles Fletcher: 'Christ's Victorie in Heaven'.

A Scottish Rhapsody

An easy way to make an Irishman angry is to tell him there is no such plant as the Shamrock. The statement, however, is disingenuous, the truth rather being that there are several Shamrocks, at least several plants with trefoil leaves that have gone by that name. The heraldic Fleur-de-lys is also a mysterious plant; nowadays it is usually identified with the Iris, but Alphonse Karr is not sure that it is a plant and not a bunch of lance-heads, or even bees. The Welshman's plant is the Leek, but some would make out it is the Daffodil. A Thistle has long been the national flower of Scotland; Dunbar wrote *The Thistle and the Rose* for James IV's wedding with the English princess; but which of the many Thistles it is, no one knows.

The distinction has been claimed for Melancholy Thistle, a plant of northern pastures with large magenta blooms and leaves that show their white undersides to the wind. The name might seem against it, but Culpeper says its name belies its nature; a decoction of it makes a man not melancholy, but merry as a cricket; Modern Writers may laugh, as he wisely remarks, *Let them laugh that win*! The plant, however, is without prickles, and so may be ruled out of account. Milk Thistle, on the other hand, is well-armed. If Mary Queen of Scots, imprisoned in the castle, saw it growing on Dumbarton Rock, one of its haunts, she may have supposed it was the national flower. That might not have prevented her from eating it, for like its relation, the Globe Artichoke, it was much used as food. Most Thistles indeed are considered nutritious; donkeys eat them, and, as Sam Weller says, 'no man never see a dead donkey'. Yet Milk Thistle is unlikely to be the national flower, for while it has curious white markings, due, it is said, to milk dropped from the Virgin Mary's breast, no such markings appear on the badge. Probably it is

Spear Thistle that most Scotsmen regard as their national flower. The farmer, it is true, slashes off its heads, but we could not expect that hardworking man to be as patriotic as a Knight of the Thistle. Yet Spear Thistle does not altogether correspond with the badge, and those who have studied the matter are generally agreed that the plant in question is Cotton Thistle, sometimes indeed called Scotch Thistle. It is a handsome plant of which Scotsmen should be proud. Unfortunately it is not a true Thistle, nor is it native to the North; the only Scotch Thistle I have seen in Scotland grew in a flower-pot at Stirling station.

Heather might have been a better national flower, but it does not lend itself to artistic treatment. Thumping his staff on the ground to emphasize his words, Scott said to Washington Irving, 'If I did not see the heather, at least once a year, *I think I should die!*' The remark was of course rhetorical, for how could he avoid seeing it a hundred times a year? When Tennyson told Carlyle he would like to see the splendours of the Brazilian forests before he died, his friend answered, 'The scraggiest bit of heath in Scotland is more to me than all the forests of Brazil'. A Scotsman takes a sentimental, almost a proprietary interest in Heather. When as a child I crossed the border into Cumberland, I felt indignant to see it growing in England. Yet Heather, like the Scots Pine, will grow almost anywhere, though it is not fond of chalk and limestone hills. Even now I feel a certain indignation when it is called Ling by English people. Who ever heard of White Ling? There would be no luck about the house if we brought home a sprig of White Ling. Ling is the name of a coarse fish, and it ought to be enough that two plants have the same name as shell-fish, Periwinkle and Cockle. If the words Heather and heathen are connected, meaning the plant and people that live on heaths, Dr Johnson would of course have agreed that the name was appropriate at least in Scotland. It is used loosely, for Bell and Cross-leaved Heath are also called Heather, but every Scotsman knows to what plant Hudson refers when he says:

Over all the revelations of the glory of flowers I have experienced in this land I hold my first sight of heather on the Scottish moors in August.[1]

1. *The Land's End.*

We cannot fail to see the Heather's flowers, for with remarkable thrift it clings to them long after they are withered and grey; but Bog Myrtle's rusty inflorescence is not so often seen, for, appearing before the leaves – natural in a wind–pollinated plant – it is soon gone to seed. As no plant has a more haunting scent, I half grudge it to England, though there, I admit, it has a pleasant name, Sweet Gale. Yet I scarcely believe it grows in England, for even in the New Forest, when I crush its leaves and close my eyes, the scent transports me to a Highland glen. Blaeberry grows in dryer places; early in autumn, scared by the thought of drought, it may drop its leaves to restrict the loss of moisture, and so present a stringy appearance. But in May or June it is a beautiful plant; its urn-shaped flowers having no need to hang and blush in the way they do. I cannot grudge it to England; it is too abundant on southern hills, where it goes by such names as Bilberry, Whinberry and Whortleberry. In any case I have a grievance against it. Climbing towards the summit of the Cobbler one July day, I was hot and thirsty, but the sun, hotter and thirstier, had been before me and drunk the runnels dry. Lying flat in a bed of Blaeberries I thrust handfuls of the purple fruit into my mouth, and, greatly refreshed, gained the summit. An hour or so later, having descended from the hill, I was walking along the road that runs round the head of the loch to Arrochar. Meeting people who smiled pleasantly to me, I smiled pleasantly to them. But they seemed unusually pleasant, and I began to wonder what was wrong. Though I knew it was nothing about my dress, for I always climb mountains in my ordinary clothes, I adjusted my tie. Their pleasantness became at last unbearable, and I darted into the Arrochar hotel. 'Who have you been kissing today?' asked the barman. 'Blaeberries', I replied, seeing in the mirror at his back the large purple stain on my mouth.

Some plants are so much of the North that they seem strayed wanderers in the South. One might imagine Dwarf Cornel had set out to meet its relation, the Cornel or Dogwood of the chalk-hills, but having reached Yorkshire fell into the Hole of Horcum and was unable to get out. That would not be surprising, for in that deep hollow buses on the road seem to be flying over our heads. Grass of Parnassus is the most admired of those plants that look more at home on a northern mountain-pasture; blooming in late summer it has no rival, and some might wonder why it should be called a Grass. Cotton-grass, a sedge, might be flattered by the name, for while Grasses, giving us corn, rice and what-not, are the most useful plants, Sedges are the most worthless. But just as Apple was a name given to any large fruit, such as Pineapple – was that why Eve's fatal fruit came to be thought an Apple? – so Grass was a name given to any herb.

A flower is the best-complexioned grass (as a pearl's the best-complexioned clay); and daily it weareth God's livery.[2]

Perhaps Grass of Parnassus is consoled by the classical allusion in its name; certainly it deserves it more than the humble Cowberry of the mountains deserves to be called by botanists Vitis Idaea, Vine of Mount Ida. Yet its flowers are fraudulent; flies, attracted by what appear to be blobs of honey, lick in vain at an empty show. In this, of course, it resembles other aspirants to the hill of the Muses.

The beauty of Grass of Parnassus strikes me as cold and passionless; I prefer other Saxifrages, and indeed any truer mountain plant. That, however, is partly due to false sentiment. One February day I set out to climb Lochnagar. Having been baffled in an attempt the day before, I was determined to succeed. After a long hard struggle with the ice-covered rocks I came in sight of the cairn. The rest of the way, a few hundred yards, was easy; yet I turned back. The white wilderness of snow appalled me; I felt the air was too cold to breathe; the cairn, with a thin mist hovering over it, was like a smoking altar on which I was about to be sacrificed. The experience has made me sympathetic with plants that live through so terrible a winter. For it is not as seeds, that can endure almost any cold, that they survive; they have too short a season to produce seeds; they are perennials. Yet my sympathy is misplaced. Snow shelters them from their greatest danger, drying winds, and being full of air – it is air between the crystals that makes it white – allows them to breathe and retain their heat, like sheep caught in a snow-drift. But who is so rational as not to feel at times what he might admit was a misplaced sympathy?

2. Fuller: *The Worthies of England*.

Mountain plants are attractive in themselves. We stop to look at Alpine Mouse-ear Chickweed, though we might not give a glance at its lowland relations. We watch the broad leaves of Alpine Lady's Mantle juggling with silver raindrops in the wind. We wonder how Roseroot, a Sedum or Plant that Sits, can cling with its rose-scented roots to the sheer side of a wet gully. Mountain Avens – not entirely a mountain plant; we can see it by Loch Assynt as well as on Ben More Assynt – shows a strange exuberance, for as its botanical name, Dryas octopetala, tells us, it has Oak-like leaves and a flower with eight petals. Rock Scorpion-grass is so blue it might have dropped from the sky. But the chief attraction of some of these mountain plants is their rareness. One plant, that grows on the Cuillins in Skye, is so rare that it was not discovered till half a century ago, and has seldom been seen since. But perhaps that particular plant would not attract many people; their chances of finding it are too small. When I told an Edinburgh botanist I was on my way to look for it, he smiled and shook his head; he had looked for it too often himself. Yet when I explained my plan, 'It's an idea', he said.

My plan was simple: I had heard of someone who had seen the plant, having been *carried* to the place; who could have been employed in that job but —, the well-known guide to the Cuillins? I would go to him and, though I had to hire him to carry me too, I would see the plant. Undoubtedly the plan was good; the only difficulty, as I learned in crossing the ferry, was that the guide had been dead for some years. The ferryman who told me this saw my disappointed look, for he went on, 'But if you want a guide, there's his brother'. His brother, a guide too! It's still an idea, I thought. So an hour or so later I stepped off the Portree bus and climbed to the cottage where, as I had been told, the brother lived with his sister. The sister opened the door and I inquired if her brother was at home. She looked at me strangely and asked if I was the minister. When I replied 'No', she asked if I was a lawyer. When I again replied 'No', she shut the door. This conduct struck me as peculiar, but there seemed nothing I could do about it; so I made my way to a cottage that offered Refreshments. Getting into conversation with the girl who laid the table, I asked if there was anything queer about the woman in the other cottage. She stared at me and said sharply, 'No, there is nothing queer about her', and left the room. I began to think there was something queer about myself. Returning a few minutes later with my ham and eggs she said in a low voice, 'She's dead'. 'Dead! when did she die?' I exclaimed. 'This morning', she replied. So it was not the sister who opened the door, but a relation or friend. As my stay in Skye was for only a few days, during which of course I could not decently call on the brother, I concluded my quest was now at an end. I was walking along the road sadly, when I heard a shout behind; a man came running up and asked if I was the gentleman who had called, and what would I be wanting. I began to apologize for having called at such a time, but 'What would you be wanting?' he insisted. When I explained it was only to inquire about a plant, he asked, 'And what would be the plant?' On my naming it, he became excited and waving his arms cried, 'It grows in Corrie —', but what corrie he said I could not make out. 'Corrie what?' I asked, but the louder he shouted, the less I could take it in. I unfolded a map and asked if he could show me the place. He stared at it hard and then, plunging his finger into the Atlantic Ocean, said, 'That's the very spot'. I thanked him and continued on my way.

That evening I lodged with a woman who gave me a salmon-trout for supper; 'Not what you're accustomed to', she said, which was true enough. When I asked about the corrie, pronouncing the name as well as I could, she shook her head; but after I had pronounced it several times with slight variations, she cried 'Oh, you mean Corrie —', and 'That's right', I said. I tried to find it on the map, but the pronunciation of Gaelic names bears little relation to the way they are spelt. I invited her to help me, but like the guide's brother she could not understand a map. She did better, however, for taking me to the door she pointed out the corrie itself, high in the mountains. Later, as I looked at it from my bedroom window, it seemed to be offering me an open invitation. 'Good night', I said, 'we shall meet to-morrow.'

In the morning I awoke to the sound of rain, and it rained all that day and the next. What takes so many tourists to Skye, I have no idea; perhaps in some way they confuse Skye with heaven. The Cuillins had vanished in mist, giving the impression it was on only a few fine days in the year they visited the island. I began to fear I might not find the plant after all. But on the third morning the sky was blue and the mountains were back in their place, looking as though they had never left it. 'A day of days', I said, as I took the road. Passing Sligachan hotel, I saw some men in awkward black clothes coming out of the bar, and I knew it was the day of the funeral. The brother, who was among them, caught sight of me and rushed forward, shouting the name of the corrie; 'You will find it', he cried and waved his arms as though with the determination that I should. 'I expect I shall', I replied. As I climbed towards the corrie a raven, hopping away from a dead sheep with a dismal bark, seemed a bad omen; but inside the corrie an eagle circled high over my head as though already crowning me with success. I began the search, crawling up the black dripping rock-ledges and sliding down the screes in a torrent of stones. I saw Stony Rock-cress, not the plant I wanted, but encouraging as its nearest relation. I almost feared to find it too soon, without a struggle worthy of the reward; but, as it turned out, I had no reason to fear. It was a long search; in fact it was already evening when I stood again at the entrance to the corrie. I looked across the sea to the distant Torridon mountains. I reflected how happy I had been one summer on those wild ridges and peaks, especially that bald-headed Ben Eighe, with no need to search for plants, there being none to find. And today I might have enjoyed myself climbing one of the Cuillins instead of looking for a plant which in the end I had not found. Why did I allow this hateful obsession of wild flowers to spoil my life? Could I not even now shake it off? 'It's an idea', I said.

But how could I have said such a thing, knowing there was one flower I could never give up? With Amaryllis I had merely flirted, but with this flower it was a different matter.

Oh, but you will tell me perhaps, that it is fantastic, to compare a man's homage to woman with his love for a flower,

writes Thomas Campbell, and having shown it is not fantastic, goes on:

Then why should I be shy to confess that my heart has a gallantry for flowers?[3]

People have fallen in love with a statue; Onomarchus of Andros, the sophist, even advised lovers how to address one:

> O unloving and unkind! To me thou hast granted not one word;[4]

but if with a statue, why not with a flower? Would it be very different from falling in love with a dryad? Did Xerxes not dote on a Plane-tree,

> that old Xerxes, when he stayed
> His march to conquest of the world?

He decked it with ornaments,

> Giving her neck its necklace, and each arm
> Its armlet, suiting soft waist, snowy side,
> With cincture and apparel.[5]

Handel's *Largo* is the air Xerxes sings to the tree in the opera. Herodotus says he left it in charge of one of the soldiers called the Immortals. And did not Passienus Crispus, a Roman consul, fall in love with a beautiful Beech, feeding its roots with wine and sleeping under it at night? Our own Chaucer too confesses his love for the Daisy:

> of this I wol nat lye,
> Ther lovèd no wight hotter in his lyve.

He shows all the signs of a lover:

> Withouten slepe, withouten mete or drynke;
> Adoun ful softèly I gan to synke,
> And lenynge on myn elbowe and my syde,
> The longè day I shoop me for to abide,
> For nothing ellis, and I shall nat lye,
> But for to loke upon the dayèsie.[6]

My flower grew on the Angus mountains; I had not even seen it, enamoured only of the name, Blue Sow-thistle. Sow-thistle

3. *Letters from the South*.
4. Philostratus: *Lives of the Sophists*.
5. Browning: 'Prince Hohenstiel-Schwangau'.
6. 'The Legende of Good Women'.

may evoke derision, suggesting a plant merely fit for pigs. Yet wise old Hecale, when Theseus was about to fight the Marathonian bull – the bull no doubt had fed on Fennel, for Marathon means Fennel – gave him a dish of Sow-thistles. In any case my flower was the Blue Sow-thistle, and Blue put a different complexion on both name and plant. People think themselves lucky if once in a blue moon they find a Blue Pimpernel, and how excited they were when Kingdon Ward discovered the Blue Poppy! What would gardeners not give for a Blue Rose? Luther Burbank said he could produce one, but he never did; probably no one will, for there seems to be no blue flower with which a Rose can be crossed. Blue stands for the more or less unattainable.

The rich blue of the unattainable flower of the sky drew my soul towards it,

says Richard Jefferies.[7] On the whole I was more reasonable than he was, for what drew my soul was this blue flower on the Angus mountains, very rare indeed, but not, I imagined, unattainable.

I knew all its relations, which of course are not blue but yellow, especially the two common Sow-thistles. They are, I admit, so alike in their stupid dullness that for anyone but a botanist to distinguish them would be a work of supererogation; this did not distress me, however, for lovers are apt to be embarrassed by the plain looks of their prospective relations. I was more attracted by Corn Sow-thistle, standing like Ruth among the corn. I had even met the very rare Marsh Sow-thistle. I was walking by the Medway, communing with dead poets who haunt its banks, Wyatt and Sir Philip Sidney, and I was so taken aback that I forgot to introduce them; otherwise I might have said, 'This is the step-sister of that heavenly blue flower you see in the Elysian Fields'.

For years I lived on the name only, Blue Sow-thistle, but at last I found myself in a village near the head of an Angus glen, the thrilling neighbourhood of the flower itself. Staying at the manse I asked the minister – it was on my first evening after supper – 'Do you know the rare flowers of the district?' I was struck by the promptness of his reply 'No', but thought little about it, as I had not supposed he would know even the common

7. *The Story of my Heart.*

ones. I had more hope of the innkeeper, who must have entertained botanists; in fact I was wondering how I could decently leave a Presbyterian manse to visit the inn, when the minister surprised me by saying he was going there himself. It appeared, however, it was only to leave the morning paper. When I said I would take a walk to the inn and leave it for him, he agreed, though I could see from his smile what he was thinking. The innkeeper mistook me for an Englishman, and that of course led to an amusing conversation. Feeling I was on a friendly footing I said, 'Do you happen to know of a flower called Blue Sow-thistle?' Most innkeepers would have been affronted by the question, but this man beamed. Then suddenly, as though remembering something, he looked grave and shook his head. Recalling the minister's prompt 'No', I suspected there was a reason behind the denial in both cases, and guessed what it was, fear of offending the gentry by sending a stranger on to the hills. In the end he admitted as much; 'The keepers will turn you back', he said. Now it was my turn to beam, for eluding gamekeepers is the one branch of botany in which I can claim some proficiency. Perhaps he was still pleased at finding I was not an Englishman; anyhow he admitted he knew of the flower, and told me where it grew. When I said 'Good night', I warmly shook his hand.

Early next morning I set off, and after an hour's walk came in sight of the shooting-lodge. That lodge, I imagined, would be my main difficulty, so I stopped to consider the situation. I felt that already I was being watched by suspicious eyes, and decided my best plan would be to approach the lodge boldly, as though on business, then dart into a plantation and come out higher up the glen. The plan succeeded admirably; but even when I was well beyond the lodge I continued to walk quickly for fear of pursuit. (Later I learnt these precautions were unnecessary, the road being a right-of-way to Braemar.) There was no difficulty about the innkeeper's directions; three or four miles farther on I recognized the deep ravine where I had to branch off and start to climb. It was a long steep climb, but I was cheered by thinking of what I should see on the mountain's plateau; I could see it in imagination already, the Blue Sow-thistle answering the blue of the sky with its heavenlier blue. I reached the ridge, but only to find another ridge. Several times I was deceived by false ridges, but at last I climbed to where nothing was left to climb. There I saw a sight I shall never forget, a dreary waste of black peat-hags, where nothing grew or could have grown but a few starved Rushes.

The following August I was back in that Angus village, though with no intention of looking for the Blue Sow-thistle, in which I had lost all interest. But meeting a botanist there, I told him of my experience. He laughed and said, 'You were within twenty yards of the plant'. 'But where was it?' I exclaimed. 'In the ravine', he replied. He described the spot, and when he added, 'But it's an ugly place, where you might easily break your neck', I merely smiled. Next morning I set off, knowing that at last I should see the Blue Sow-thistle. This time I did not climb to the plateau, where the innkeeper, listening to botanists' talk, imagined it grew; I stopped at the spot where I had to descend into the ravine. But was it necessary to descend? I could see it from where I was, a dull-looking plant, very different from all I had dreamed. Perhaps I have no gallantry for flowers, for I decided not to break my neck.

23   The Fall

'Ripest when th'are green', says Campion of kisses, but he could not have said it of fruits. Unripe fruits are green, hiding themselves among the green leaves; as they ripen they change in colour, and we see

> The blushing Apple, bashfull Peare
> And shame-fac'd Plum, (all simp'ring there).[1]

This modesty is of course assumed; they seek now to attract the eye.

Two common colours in fleshy fruits (usually found in hedges where birds resort) are purple and black, as in Wild Plum and Blackberry; but the commonest colour is red, as in Cherries and Raspberries, Hips and Haws. The spindle-tree's crimson fruit,

> Which in our winter woodland looks a flower,[2]

splits open like a slashed sleeve, disclosing its golden seeds. Hazelnuts, the wild ancestors of Filberts and Cobs, turn brown as though tanned by the sun. Snowberry, an American shrub now abundant in plantations, has a staring white fruit; but that is unusual, if not unique, for White Currants and White Raspberries, as we call them, are yellow. Even our cultivated green fruits, Grapes and Greengages, are different in shade from the leaves, though one imagines they were Purple Grapes Zeuxis so cunningly painted,

> That the hungry birds did muster
> Round the counterfeited cluster.[3]

1. Herrick: 'To Phillis'.
2. Tennyson: 'A Dedication'.
3. Wither: 'Faire Virtue'.

The wax-coating that gives its bloom to Plum and polished surface to Hip, though attractive to us, may serve only to keep out damp, and with damp, bacteria and fungi; when we rub the bloom from a Grape, it soon, as we say, goes bad. A few fruits, especially Raspberries, have a pleasant scent, but it seems too faint to be of much use. Certainly we could not live like the inhabitants of that island visited by Mandeville, entirely on the scent of Wild Apples.

Ripening fruits change not only in colour but in taste. Like the waters of Marah, into which Moses flung the tree, their juices turn from bitter to sweet. Crab-apples may be as sour to us as the famous Herba Sardonia, of which it is said:

> It screws the mouth in a gape, so that those who are poisoned by it die with a smile on their face;[4]

the word crabbed is connected with Crab, as Sardonic is with that Sardinian plant; but no doubt even Crab-apples are sweet to some creatures. If we cannot live on them, not even on their scent, other fruits offer us a meal. George Gissing says of Blackberries he found on a country walk:

> I picked and ate, and ate on, until I had come within sight of an inn where I might have made a meal. But my hunger was satisfied; I had no need for anything more, and, as I thought of it, a strange feeling of surprise, a sort of bewilderment, came upon me. What! Could it be that I had eaten, and eaten sufficiently, *without paying*?[5]

The change from bitter to sweet in fruits appeared so wonderful to St Augustine that he compared it with the miracle of Cana in Galilee:

> For He who made wine on that day at the marriage-feast, in those six water-pots, which He commanded to be filled with water, the self-same does this every year in vines. But we do not wonder at it, because it happens every year.[6]

Trees and shrubs use fleshy, or at least edible, fruits to scatter their seeds. It is not desirable that young plants should grow up beneath their parents; the parents might overlay them with their

4. Solinus: *Memorabilia*.
5. *Private Papers of Henry Ryecroft*.
6. *Tractate on St John's Gospel*.

shade, or, absorbing the soil water, take, so to speak, the food out of their mouths. They too might suffer when the young plants grew up. Rousseau disposed of his children by carrying them out of the house to become foundlings; plants dispose of theirs in much the same way. (Seeds may be said to be children, being complete plants, with root, stem and leaf.) Some plants shoot them out, the seed-vessel acting either as a pop-gun or as a squirt.

There is a Plant called *Noli me tangere*, says Coles, near which if you put your hand, the Seed will spurtle forth suddenly, in so much that the unexpectednesse of it made the valiant Lord *Fairfax* to start, as Master *Robert* at the Physick Garden at *Oxford* can tell you.

That is why it is called Noli-me-tangere or Touch-me-not. Gorse among shrubs adopts this method. Other plants depend on the wind; perhaps it was Thistledown that made Anaxagoras imagine all seeds originated in the air. Trees, more than low less-exposed shrubs, depend on the wind that in spring may have helped to fertilize them by carrying pollen. Usually the seeds, or it may be the fruits, are so fitted out that they do not readily fall, but are borne to a distance; the seeds of Pine and Birch are winged, and the Willow's seeds, which live for only a few days, are feathered. Most trees and shrubs, however, count on animals, tempting them with fruits. Few wild fruits tempt us; yet, if we could believe the poet,

> Time was, that while the autumn fall did last,
> Our hungry sires gaped for the falling mast.
> Could no unhuskèd acorn leave the tree,
> But there was challenge made whose it might be.
> And if some nice and lickerous appetite
> Desired more dainty dish of rare delight,
> They scaled the storèd crab with claspèd knee,
> Till they had sated their delicious eye;
> Or searched the hopeful thicks of hedgy-rows,
> For briary berries, or haws, or sourer sloes.[7]

Perhaps they found Beech-mast the most nourishing; of Aaron Hill we are told:

7. Joseph Hall: 'Virgidemiarum'.

He undertook to make an oil, as sweet as that from olives, from beech-nuts, and obtained a patent for the purpose;[8]

and Johns tells of a man who had a scheme for paying off the National Debt by that means. But I doubt if trees and shrubs ever regarded human beings as of much use in the world; they look more to other animals. Rooks and squirrels carry off Acorns, and if the rook's appetite fails or the squirrel forgets about its hoard, a young Oak may arise, spreading in time broad branches on which their distant descendants may perch or play. Starlings alight on a Gean, and as they eat the Cherries, the slippery stones fly from their bills. Though maybe

'Tis not for gravity to play at cherry-pit,[9]

children know how easily the stones shoot from their fingers. The one great occasion when we helped a tree was when Adam and Eve, eating the Apple, flung away the core; the tree must have propagated itself, for we still eat of the same forbidden fruit.

Some trees hasten to drop their ripened fruits. Beneath a Horse Chestnut, still in full foliage, the fruits, like small green hedgehogs, lie thick on the ground. (What are the brown varnished seeds for? Children play a game with them, and I always carry one in my pocket; but who ever sees a seedling tree?) We may take shelter under a leafy Oak, only to face a shower of thudding Acorns. But other trees cling to their fruits long after the leaves have fallen. Scarlet Hips, 'coffins of the dead dog-rose', are like Mohammed's coffin suspended in the air; no doubt to birds they are more conspicuous on the bare branches than lying in the grass. The Ash clings so long to its Keys, winged fruits, that it might be keeping them for Janus to unlock the new year; perhaps it is waiting for the stronger winds of winter to bear them farther. We think of leaves, not of fruits, when we speak of the fall.

Unless they are peculiar in some way, thick-skinned as in Holly, or mere needles as in Scots Pine, leaves are a disadvantage in winter. Though the Larch has but small leaves – '*leaves* it cannot be said to have', says Wordsworth,[10] who hated the tree

8. Johnson: *Lives of the Poets.*
9. *Twelfth Night.*
10. *Guide to the Lakes.*

so much that he flung his hat at some seedlings[11] – yet, shedding
them in autumn, it can live on colder mountains than Scots Pine.
A tree in full leaf would be top-heavy in a winter gale; and snow
might be an even greater danger. Trees covered, not with their
own foliage, but with Ivy's, often fall in a blizzard. Ivy with its
leafy screen protected the infant Bacchus from his step-mother,
Hera, but it is far from protecting a tree from Boreas. When it
embraces a tree, –

> Nay, seems to say, dear tree, we shall not part,
> In sign whereof, lo! in each leaf a heart –[12]

though it does not, as Prospero thought, suck verdure out on't,
it may with the weight of snow bring down the tree and itself in
a common ruin, as Samson brought down the house of Dagon.
A tree cannot divorce its Ivy-wife; but it can shed its own
leaves.

Trees have a stronger reason for getting rid of their leaves. In
dry hot lands they shed them, not in autumn, but in spring; in
fact, they may be said to hibernate in summer. Their fear is
drought, the leaves evaporating more water than the roots can
supply. Our trees too are afraid of drought; an Elm, it is said,
may have seven million leaves, capable of losing seven tons of
water in a day; but their drought would come in winter, when
the roots, lying like sluggish serpents, can scarcely act in the cold
soil. Though a major operation, it is a sign of health when a tree
makes a full sweep of its foliage; usually they are weak young
trees, or trees mutilated in hedges, that have withered leaves
clinging to them through winter. Winds do not rob a tree; they
are merely scavengers. A tree is its own surgeon, or, as Dante
says, the leaves fall of themselves:

> Come d'autumno si levan le foglie
> L'una appresso dell' altra, infin che il ramo
> Vede alla terra tutte le sue spoglie.[13]

Each wound is sealed with cork to prevent evaporation and keep
out bacteria; the purpose cork also serves in a wine-bottle. Trees
toy with their leaves in June:

11. De Quincey: *Lake Reminiscences*.
12. Drummond: 'Sonnet xxxvii'.
13. *Inferno*.

> Here waving groves a chequer'd scene display,
> And part admit, and part exclude the day;
> As some coy nymph her lover's warm address
> Not quite indulges, nor can quite repress;[14]

but in autumn they find them an expense. If they make a more splendid display with them, it is only

> As a rich beauty, when her bloom is lost,
> Appears with more magnificence and cost.[15]

Trees look supernatural in their strength; yet any tree is more than half dead already, its inner wood mere timber, which a hollow Oak or Yew lives well enough without. And we can imagine they are tired in autumn. Oaks especially, like those Oaks that came to be

> Transplanted to the Mountains of the Waves,[16]

show signs of heavy weather and fighting. Their heavy weather was calm summer days, and their foes insects. Though well protected against a tree's worst foes, bacteria and fungi – the tannin that protects them is used to protect our shoes – they suffer in summer from hundreds of kinds of insects. How numerous one of these may be we learn as we stand under an Oak in June and listen to a pattering sound, steady as rain but thinner and harder; caterpillars, that feed on the leaves, are dropping their tiny dung. They can almost strip the tree; fortunately, at the time they change to green moths that alight on our clothes, the Oak produces a second crop of leaves, Lammas-shoots they are called, making light patches on the darker foliage, a little spring in midsummer. Later on we notice the various galls, Oak-apples and Oak-spangles, 'bastard fruits', due to an irritation set up by a grub. Other plants show these abnormal growths, the Bedeguar or Robin's-cushion in a Briar, and, caused by a fungus, the Witch's broom in a Birch, and in a Sycamore inky stains on the leaves. Insects may seem small foes, but it was to gnats that Homer compared the persistent Trojans. How persistently they attack may be seen when flies are caught

14. Pope: 'Windsor Forest'.
15. Crabbe: 'Adventures of Richard'.
16. *Liber Plantarum*.

in amber. Hoping perhaps to lay their young in the broken limb of a Pine, they are caught in the resin the tree pours over the wound. So clearly are they caught in the attempt, we might imagine that though the resin has long been fossilized as amber, they still persist in their hope; but

> Safe in their alabaster chambers
> Untouched by morning and untouched by noon,
> Sleep the meek members of the resurrection.[17]

All trees feel the strain of summer. Beneath an Elm we may see twigs, not torn off by the wind, but actively cast away, the straitened tree seeking to preserve its strength. To produce flowers and seeds is itself a strain; in the Horse Chestnut the twigs that bear them die of exhaustion. Autumn must seem a blessed time for trees, when the wicked cease from troubling and the weary are at rest. They have laid up a store of food, and will be ready, when spring awakes them, to burst into foliage. Fat as an autumn bear and clad in a new overcoat of bark (usually they wear their old overcoats as well, creased or, as we say, wrinkled) they settle down to their winter sleep,

> Full of sweet dreams, and health, and quiet breathing.[18]

It is not cold they have to fear, but rather an unnatural and disturbing warmth. An icy wind they will wrap about them like a blanket. So Robert Frost, farmer as well as poet, warns his Apple trees in autumn:

> How often already you've had to be told,
> Keep cold, young orchard. Good-bye and keep cold.[19]

17. Emily Dickinson.
18. Keats: 'Endymion'.
19. 'Good-Bye and Keep Cold'.

24 The Year's Last Flower

Driving one day with a friend over the Surrey Downs I happened to remark, 'I have never seen Ground Pine'. This curious chalk-hill plant, though a kind of Bugle, looks like a small Pine; and it has the scent of one, a scent so unforgettable that formerly it was called Forget-me-not. Anne Pratt says it blooms in April and May, Johns in May and June. Having sought it in vain for several years, I was excited when my friend said, 'I can show you a field where it grows; I can take you there now'. He drove me along a lane, and stopping by a gate, said, 'This is the field'. I was already climbing the gate when he asked where I was going. 'To look for Ground Pine', I replied. 'It will take you a long time to find it', he said. Measuring the small field with my eye and thinking in terms of minutes, 'How long?' I asked. 'About three months', he replied, adding as I stared in astonishment, 'It does not bloom till September'. I wonder if Anne Pratt or Johns had seen Ground Pine.

Most plants have gone to seed by September:

> The smoke of the traveller's joy is puffed
> Over hawthorn berry and hazel tuft,[1]

the smoke being long-feathered fruits that the wind will blow farther than most smoke. Or perhaps the seeds are already buried, their sextons rain and worms and drifting leaves. Flowers left by summer are still plentiful in the fields, but butterflies – Peacock, Red Admiral and Tortoiseshell – are forsaking them for gardens. Dogwood, its leaves blushing in an extraordinary manner, may have started to bloom again; Herb Robert may be in flower and fruit at the same time, like Aaron's rod that 'brought forth buds, and bloomed blossoms, and yielded almonds'. The Bramble,

1. Edward Thomas: 'The Sign-Post'.

too, as we pick Blackberries, is still wearing its white roses, showing the old vanity that made it say to the trees in Jotham's parable, 'come and put your trust in my shadow'. But we hardly expect a flower to make its first appearance in September.

Yet autumn has a trick of repeating some of the notes of spring, like a person who cannot get Mendelssohn's *Spring Song* out of his head.

> Autumn has come like spring returned to us,
> Won from her girlishness; like one returned
> A friend that was a lover.[2]

Yellow and blue are the predominant colours in autumn, as they were before the red, purple and white of summer – yellow the stronger, though Toadflax, Fleabane and Ragwort are not names for poets to conjure with as when, evoking the spirit of spring, they conjured with Primrose, Daffodil and Bluebell. It is not uncommon to find a Violet in September; occasionally, too, a Wild Rose in a hedge

> Hangs, a pale mourner for the summer past,
> Making a little summer where it grows.[3]

Autumnal Gorses are in full bloom in the South and West, dwarf plants, often mistaken for small bushes of common Gorse. Meadow Saffron, a poisonous Lily, looks so much like a Crocus that it gives us a start of surprise to meet it in September; the leaves came in early summer, but they have withered away, the flower appearing like a posthumous poem. Autumn Squill on western sea-cliffs makes us think with regret of the days when we saw Spring Squill.

That we should have Crocuses in Spring and also in autumn seemed strange to White of Selborne:

> This circumstance is one of the wonders of creation.

Yet conditions in autumn are not so different from those of spring. It was with no thought, however, of seeing a Crocus, that I travelled one September day to Saffron Walden. (I remembered how I had seen, earlier in the year, Purple Spring Crocus;

2. Browning: 'Pauline'.
3. Hartley Coleridge: 'November'.

for it grew not many miles away, in private grounds, the only plant to which I have been conducted by a family butler.) Sheltering from rain in the Museum, I heard a voice, 'I see you are interested in archaeology', and found myself talking to the curator. An archaeologist himself, he began, starting from the earliest times, to discourse on ancient history. 'By the way,' I said, staving off an imminent invasion by the Romans, 'does Saffron Crocus still survive about Saffron Walden?' The effect of my question was astonishing; dragged back from the mists of time to a damper September afternoon, he suddenly changed to a botanist. 'It does, indeed', he cried, 'and this is the time to see it. If you go to the Quakers' School and ask for Mr —, one of the masters, he will show it to you.' So I turned up my coat-collar and set off for the Quakers' School. It was still within school-hours when I arrived there, but understanding it was a principle with Quakers to reward evil with good, I rang the bell. Yet my footsteps echoed with a guilty sound as the porter led me along an empty corridor. He knocked at a door and ushered me into a room full of boys. They sprang to their feet with 'Good-afternoon, sir', and 'Good-afternoon', I replied. Then the little wretches sat down, all eyes fixed on the wet stranger, all ears open to learn the object of his visit. I felt nervous, but my visit might have been part of the school curriculum, the master took it so smilingly. 'Boys, get on with your work, while I attend to this gentleman', he said, and we left the room together. Rain was now pouring down almost as hard as it does in a film, but we dashed across the grounds to where, its purple flames unperturbed by rain, he showed me the plant that gave its name to Saffron Walden.

Perhaps I should write a book about Saffron Crocus, for from that time I took a great interest in the plant. The book would deal of course with the curious case of the crocodile. Crocodile means Crocus-dreader, says Fuller, and explains that the creature dreads the plant as an antidote to its poison; in fact, only when it is taken to a place where Saffron Crocus grows are the reptile's tears genuine. Yet if it so dreads the Crocus because of its name, we might feel sorry for it, misled, like Fuller, by a false etymology. Probably the book would also quote the case of Propertius, who thought it a sign of degeneracy that the Roman stage so reeked of saffron, yet, on going to a banquet, prayed that his hair might be three times bathed with Cilician saffron. That would lead to telling how Italian ladies dyed their hair with saffron, though priests warned them that the flame-like colour presaged the fires of Purgatory. How the plant was introduced into this country would be told as Hakluyt relates it in *Remembrances for master S., who was going to trade in Turkie*:

It is reported at Saffronwalden that a Pilgrim proposing to do good to his countrey, stole an head of Saffron, and hid the same in his Palmers staffe, which he made hollow before of purpose, and so he brought this root into this realme, with venture of his life; for if he had bene taken, by the law of the countrey from whence it came, he had died for the fact.

The book would deal with the extensive cultivation of the plant, when a pound of saffron was worth a pound of money. Evelyn need not have travelled as far as Saffron Walden to see 'that useful plant, with which all the country is covered'; is there not a Saffron Hill in London? A chapter would be taken up with a description of a wrestling-match in Cornwall, at which, carried away by excitement, I bought and tasted – though only tasted – a saffron cake. But can I conscientiously write this book, if I have never seen a Saffron Crocus? Travelling one day in a train I fell into conversation with a man who told me he came from Saffron Walden. Staring hard at him, I asked, 'Do you remember one wet September day, about ten years ago, sending me from the Museum to the Quakers' School to see Saffron Crocus?' 'I have no recollection of it, but probably I did', he replied; 'anyhow you did not see it'. 'Oh, yes, I did', I said with a smile. But he shook his head; 'No, I made a mistake about the plant; what you saw was not Saffron Crocus but Naked Ladies'. Perhaps, for the good name of the Quakers' School, I should explain that by Naked Ladies he meant Naked-flowering Crocus.

But Ground Pine, Naked Ladies and Saffron Crocus are not alone in September. The stubbles are full of flowers, especially Mayweeds, looking like middle-sized sisters of Oxeye and Daisy: the Mayweed called Scentless, though it is aromatic, and False Camomile that, as the season advances, impudently thrusts out its golden breast. These Mayweeds have nothing to do with the month of May, the name meaning that they cure mays or young women. Chicory's blue flowers at the field's edge reproach the fading September sky; other flowers are shades of blue, Chicory's flower is blue itself. Root-fields are even richer in flowers, and no wonder; for, crafty enough not to appear before the farmer's hoe singles the Turnips, they live on the fat of the land. We might grudge it to Petty Spurge and White Goosefoot, sometimes called Fat Hen or Dirty Dick; but what a sight a Swede-field is in the North, full of Marigolds and Variegated Hemp-nettles, and of course the Swedes themselves, like great purple skulls that have burst into foliage. Lilac-whorled Mints are abundant, but growing in ditches they may not affect us as the sight of Mint affected Gerard:

It doth stir up the minde and the taste to a greedie desire of meete.

It is strange they live in ditches, for almost all their aromatic relations, such as Thyme, Basil and Rosemary, prefer dry places; but these have withered away, all except Wood-betony by the side of the road. Orpine and Tansy might claim to be the year's last flower, for Orpine is sometimes called Livelong, and Tansy is short for Athanasia or Immortality. Hung in houses, as it often was, Orpine would live long, for its leaves are stored with water like a camel's stomach, food laid by, not for a rainy day, but a dry day. Tansy on the other hand – its name is a mystery – is short-lived, and can hardly hope now to survive in a Tansy-cake. Mountain Everlasting might as well be called the year's last flower; better indeed, being an immortelle. But perhaps the best flower to take leave of the year with, if one were fortunate to find it, would be Marsh Gentian, sometimes called Calathian Violet. Gentius, King of Illyria, who discovered the virtue of Gentians, was not clad in such colour; its tube is of so deep a blue, that as one gazes down, inches change to fathoms.

As all these plants begin to bloom in August, if not before, none should claim to be the year's last flower, if we mean by that the year's last effort. And that is what we must mean; otherwise Chickweed, Groundsel and Shepherd's-purse, rejected as the year's first flower, might claim now to be its last. So it appears that like Paris confronted with the pretensions of the three goddesses, Hera, Athene and Aphrodite, we must choose among Ground Pine, Saffron Crocus and Naked Ladies. Perhaps, not unlike Paris, we might incline to favour Naked Ladies, but a complication occurs. Driving back that day from the field where Ground Pine grows, my friend warned me of another flower not to be expected before September, Cyclamen. Its more English name is Sowbread, and though we have no wild boars to dig up its roots, it may, for all we know, be a native. Yet when I invited a lady who made a hobby of wild flowers to take me in her car to Hawkhurst to see this rare plant, she flatly refused, scorning the idea that Cyclamen grew wild in this country. I persuaded her in the end; but, half-hearted from the start, when she lost her way she also lost her temper. Though I could not follow her train of thought, this seemed to convince her more than ever that Cyclamen was not wild. So it was with some satisfaction that at the end of an erratic journey I pointed to the plant growing on a bank and said 'Well?' Perhaps the word was unwise, for it stimulated her, stout as she was, to climb the bank and look over a hedge. 'Come here,' she commanded, and when I reached the top, I found myself staring at a garden lawn dotted with the pink flowers. 'So this is what you brought me to see, a garden escape', she said. I explained that so far from the Cyclamen having escaped from the garden to the bank, it had probably escaped from the bank to the garden; but my explanation did not appear convincing. As we drove back I reverted to the subject, but it would have been better to leave ill alone; once again she had lost her way.

Ground Pine, Saffron Crocus, Naked Ladies and Cyclamen: to say which of these is the year's last flower would need the judgment of a Solomon. Even he might fail if he were no better a botanist than Bacon, who describes his work as

a natural history of all verdure, from the cedar upon the mountain to the moss upon the wall, which is but a rudiment between putrefaction and an herb.[4]

But just when the problem seems beyond human solution, Bacchus descends as god from the machine, his brows wreathed with Ivy. We hail the sign! Perhaps because it is an evergreen,

> And, careless of life's passing hour,
> Its endless summer keeps,[5]

4. *Advancement of Learning*.
5. Clare: 'Life, Death, and Eternity'.

we forgot the Ivy. Yet it blooms in late autumn, seldom before October, hanging out its pale clusters of flowers to the sunlight, Bacchus nodding to Apollo. Insects do not forget. 'Good wine needs no bush', they said to themselves all through the flowery summer; but now the Ivy-bush betokens wine, as when a branch of it hung outside an Elizabethan tavern. Sometimes a bee finds himself unfit to go home to his queen, and

> drunken with a thousand healths
> Of love and kind regard for flowers,
> He says in wine,
> 'Boo to her shrine!'[6]

When the plague visited Athens during the Peloponnesian War, many people, says Thucydides,

resolved to enjoy themselves while they could and think of nothing but pleasure.

It was during a plague that Boccaccio's tales were told. So when the autumn's leaves are fleeing,

> Yellow, and black, and pale, and hectic red,
> Pestilence-stricken multitudes,[7]

insects have their final fling. The Ivy's bloom is for them the last flower of their lives; for us perhaps it is only the year's last flower.

6. W. H. Davies: 'A Drinking Song'.
7. Shelley: 'Ode to the West Wind'.

Apologia

One morning, coming down to breakfast in a Peterborough hotel, I looked out of the window, and to a man already seated at the table said, 'Do you think it will keep up?' 'What will keep up?' he asked, and added, 'I suppose you are a Scotsman and are talking about the weather'. I confided that I was on my first visit to the South and, as though that needed an explanation, that I had come to look at old churches. 'Going to be an architect?' he asked. 'No, it's just to look at them', I said. 'Don't talk to me about old churches', he cried; 'I have seen all the old churches in England'. I thought it strange, for he did not look like a man with a passion for Gothic Architecture; yet, when I joined him at the table, I found that he had indeed seen many churches, and had travelled far and wide to see them. But what made it stranger still was that he appeared to have little appreciation of what he had seen. The matter would have remained a mystery, had I not met him a few days later at Stamford; there I learnt that his business was taking photographs for picture-postcards.

The reason I recall him now is that my knowledge of plants may seem like his knowledge of churches. I almost think so myself when I consider the botanist's knowledge. Hooker tells us that when he was still a child in petticoats, his mother came on him grubbing in a wall and asked what he was doing.

I cried out that I had found *Bryum argenteum* (which it was not), a very pretty little moss I had seen in my father's collection.

I have not advanced so far as Hooker in his petticoats; I could not identify a Moss, even wrongly. As for the various Grasses, I could say with the Clown in *All's Well that Ends Well*, 'I am no great Nebuchadnezzar, sir; I have not much skill in grass'.

Hooker's father was Professor of Botany in Glasgow, but his predecessors in that chair were Professors of Anatomy as well, so that they had to dissect not only plants but also bodies provided by the hangman; I would as soon do the one as the other. What if the plants were still alive? Is a living plant not more than a dead body? When Asiaticus committed suicide,

he opened his veins, but not till he had inspected his funeral pyre and directed its removal to another spot, lest the smoke should hurt the thick foliage of the trees.[1]

Marco Polo discovered an island where the inhabitants ate no vegetables till they were dry, believing they had souls; probably I am a strayed descendant of those islanders. Clearly I was not born to be a botanist, and 'Never attempt to straighten out a crooked bough', says Menander. I must pray to St Teresa to make me like herself, conscious of my ignorance, but turning it to some account; as she says,

I do not understand how this is, and not understanding it gives me great consolation; for truly the soul is not so much to consider and respect her God in the things which it seems we may comprehend by our poor intellect, as in those things which we cannot in any way comprehend.[2]

Anyhow, I have enjoyed my acquaintance with plants; if botanists are rewarded according to their greater desert, even the student, scribbling his notes in the lecture-room or poring over his Strasburger at home, must find his happiness heaped-up and running over. I look back on experiences so pleasant that I am tempted to share with Keats what was to him a favourite speculation,

that we shall enjoy ourselves hereafter by having what we call happiness on Earth repeated in a finer tone.[3]

Like my great namesake, the author of *Night Thoughts*, I sigh

O for yesterdays to come!

Meanwhile by writing about these experiences I try in some measure to relive them.

1. Tacitus: *Annals*.
2. *Conceptions of Divine Love*.
3. *Letters*.

And is his ardour vain, Lorenzo? No;
That more than miracle the gods indulge;
Today is yesterday returned.

Yet looking back on my chases after plants, my conscience is troubled. I can imagine the simple Nature-lover shaking his head and saying, 'What mountebank method of studying wild flowers is this? Why this rushing after a flower for no better reason than that it is rare? Why this going to and fro in the earth, and walking up and down in it? Wisdom is before him that hath understanding, but the eyes of a fool are in the ends of the earth'. And I feel the more conscience-stricken because

> The pansy at my feet
> Doth the same tale repeat.[4]

'Let no flower in spring pass us by', says the Wisdom of Solomon. But too often flowers in spring have passed me by, neglected for some rarer plant. Primrose, Speedwell and Daisy, I have even turned from them, fearing their reproachful looks. I confess they do not mean to me what they once meant. Perhaps Jacob Boehme's experience in seeing the *very* herbs and grass is not so exceptional; I have seen flowers look at me as I looked at them, with the light and speech of living eyes. Others have had the same experience, but I fancy it is one that passes. Perhaps that is a penalty we pay for growing old, or at least for not remaining young; more likely it is the price of having eaten with Adam of the 'forbidden learned tree'. All I can say to those reproachful flowers is what Clare said to the Cowslip:

> But I'm no more akin to thee,
>   A partner of the spring;
> For time has had a hand with me,
>   And left an alter'd thing.[5]

It is to the simple Nature-lover I address my Apologia.

One evening, rowing from Grantchester to Cambridge, I was caught in a heavy shower.

4. Wordsworth: 'Ode on Intimations of Immortality'.
5. 'To the Cowslip'.

O bruit doux de la pluie
Par terre et sur les toits![6]

but sitting in an open boat I felt the rain on the river was superfluous. It did not damp, however, the spirits of some young people coming behind me in a punt. They chattered like sparrows in the rain; indeed, the sky was blue again before they realized the shower was past. Then a girl said, 'It's stopped raining'; to which a young man replied, 'So it has; three cheers for Nature!'

Now I do not profess to be a Nature-lover like those young people in the punt; I did not join in the cheers, nor did I enjoy the rain. Yet I am perplexed; for if they loved Nature so much, how did they manage to put up with one another's company? I crave to be alone with Nature, on the principle, I suppose, that two is company and three none. The presence of a friend on a country walk makes me uncomfortable; I even try to avoid strangers. Two lovers in a lane of course are different; I feel that they and myself are occupied in much the same way. As for my objection to the rain as I sat in an open boat, that was merely a lovers' quarrel. As a rule I prefer a wet or misty day, as more likely to leave me alone with Nature. People who say they do not like the country in bad weather seem to be as unreasonable as a man who should say he did not love his wife because she had a cold. If Nature is not at her best in bad weather, though she often is, to be with her then is like a husband's privilege.

So it appears I must trust to my own experience. It was wild flowers, 'children of the bountiful earth', who introduced me to Nature, Persephone shyly leading me to her Mother. Like the Luck-flower of the legend, they opened a magic door. As I entered I had the sense of a Presence. It was not the theological experience that Scupoli describes:

When you notice trees, grass and such-like things, by your under-standing you will see that the life which they live, they have not of themselves, but from the spirit which you do not see, and which alone gives them life.[7]

Nor had it anything to do with the beauty of a particular object or a fair landscape. How often I have said,

6. Verlaine: *Ariettes oubliées*.
7. *The Spiritual Combat*.

Though all men of earth's beauty speak,
Beauty here I do not seek
More than I sought it on my mother's cheek.

Nor was it the rarer sense of something shining through, making the earth look spiritual, as I saw it from Canisp. I felt it rather in a dim wood, and most of all in a mountain mist – a sense of nearness, but without any idea of what I was near to. In a mountain mist, lost to the world, I might have said:

This is the *cloud of unknowing*; this is Denis' divinity, his lightsome darkness and unknown knowing.[8]

I might even have said:

This is the dark silence, in which all lovers lose themselves.[9]

Yet I am far from thinking I shared the experience of the mystics. If I felt the earth was a haunted place, I had no idea by whom it was haunted. I was even suspicious of the experience.

When St Paul saw nothing he saw God; when Elias wrapped his face in his mantle, God came,

says Tauler; but he goes on:

Those who see in this way, with undue liberty and false light, are in a perilous state.[10]

Now at least, I have no desire for anything outside the Catholic tradition. We comprehend with all saints. 'If thou knowest not, O thou fairest among women, go thy way forth by the footsteps of the flock.'

But I must not forget my Apologia to the simple Nature-lover, to whom I appear as Satan from going to and fro in the earth, and from walking up and down in it. When I preached my first sermon, the man with whom I was staying – I still remember he was a veterinary surgeon – said, 'You did well enough, but let me give you a piece of advice; next time you enter the pulpit, do not climb the stair two steps at a time'. A restless spirit may account for my running after rare flowers, but it must be admitted that

8. *Epistle of Privy Counsel* (unknown writer).
9. Ruysbroeck: *The Adornment of the Spiritual Marriage*.
10. *Sermons*.

seldom have I attempted to discover them myself. So I have had the more leisure to sit on a boulder or a fallen tree-trunk and think of other things. The simple Nature-lover should believe Wordsworth, when he says:

> His simple truths did Andrew glean
> Beside the babbling rills;
> A careful student he had been
> Among the woods and hills.[11]

11. 'The Oak and the Broom'.